BOTH
OF THE STORY

100 *ALL-NEW* ORIGINAL AUDITION MONOLOGUES

by

JASON MILLIGAN

SAMUEL FRENCH, INC.

45 West 25th Street   7623 Sunset Boulevard
NEW YORK 10010   HOLLYWOOD 90046
LONDON   *TORONTO*

Copyright © 2004 by Jason Milligan

ALL RIGHT RESERVED

CAUTION: Professionals and amateurs are hereby warned that BOTH SIDES OF THE STORY is subject to a royalty. It is fully protected under the copyright laws of the United States of America, the British Commonwealth, including Canada, and all other countries of the Copyright Union. All rights, including professional, amateur, motion pictures, recitation, lecturing, public reading, radio broadcasting, television, and the rights of translation into foreign languages are strictly reserved. In its present form the play is dedicated to the reading public only.

The amateur live stage performance rights to BOTH SIDES OF THE STORY are controlled exclusively by Samuel French, Inc. and royalty arrangements and licenses must be secured well in advance of presentation. PLEASE NOTE that amateur royalty fees are set upon application in accordance with your producing circumstances. When applying for a royalty quotation and license please give us the number of performances intended, dates of production, your seating capacity and admission fee. Royalties are payable one week before the opening performance of the play to Samuel French, Inc., at 45 W. 25th. Street, New York, NY 10010: or at 7623 Sunset Blvd., Hollywood, CA 90046, or to Samuel French (Canada), Ltd., 100 Lombard Street, Lower Level, Toronto, Ontario, Canada M5C 1M3.

Royalty of the required amount must be paid whether the play is presented for charity or gain and whether or not admission is charged.

Stock royalty quoted on application to Samuel French, Inc.

For all rights other than those stipulated above, apply to Samuel French, Inc., at 45 W. 25th. Street, New York, NY 10010.

Particular emphasis is laid on the question of amateur or professional reading, permission and terms for which must be secured in writing from Samuel French, Inc.

Copyright from this book is whole or in part is strictly forbidden by law, and the right of performance is not transferable.

Whenever the play is produced the following notice must appear on all programs, printing and advertising for the play: "Produced by special arrangement with Samuel French, Inc."

Due authorship credit must be given on all programs, printing and advertising for the play.

ISBN 0 573 60263 8   Printed in U.S.A.   #4936

No one shall commit or authorize any act or omission by which the copyright of, or the right to copyright, this play be impaired.

No one shall make any changes in this play for the purpose of production.

Publication of this play does not imply availability for performance. Both amateurs and professionals considering a production are *strongly* advised in their own interests to apply to Samuel French, Inc. for written permission before starting rehearsals, advertising, or booking a theatre.

No part of this book may be reproduced, stored in a retrieval system, or transmitted in any form, by any means, now known or yet to invented, including mechanical, electronic, photocopying, recording, videotaping, or otherwise, without the prior written permission of the publisher.

IMPORTANT BILLING AND CREDIT REQUIREMENTS

All producers of *BOTH SIDES OF THE STORY must* give credit to the Author of the Play in all programs distributed in connection with performances of the Play and in all instances in which the title of the Play appears for purposes of advertising, publicizing or otherwise exploiting the Play and/or a production. The name of the Author *must* appear on a separate line on which no other name appears, immediately following the title, and *must* appear in size of type not less than fifty percent the size of the title type.

FOREWORD

I have had the privilege of writing many of Samuel French's monologue books for over fifteen years now ... and I can honestly say that I have truly enjoyed writing each and every audition piece I've ever created. I have always strived to make sure that each speech is self-contained - that the listener can easily discern the situation and circumstances from the text and performance.

However, for this collection, I'm taking one step further in this direction ... for this entire anthology is comprised of *pairs* of monologues.

On the *even*-numbered pages, you will find a brand-new, original audition piece ... and, immediately to the right, on the *odd*-numbered pages, you'll find an opposing point of view. It might be a response from the unseen character to whom the first person was speaking ... or an entirely different point of view altogether. It might be a man or a woman, the order of the sexes is mixed up throughout the book (although there are 50 pieces for woman and 50 pieces for men contained herein).

even-numbered pages
offer one point of view

odd-numbered pages
offer another on the
same topic

Either way, the pieces are all designed to stand on their own. I'm merely hoping that this new form will offer you a bit more "backstory" to work from as you prepare your monologues for performance. And, as always, feel free, whenever appropriate, to choose a piece designed for someone of the opposite gender - it may work just fine for you!

One small technical note ... throughout these pieces, I consider a "beat" to be a slight pause and a "pause" to be a longer, more significant pause.

Break-a-leg ... and enjoy!

- Jason Milligan
Fall, 2004

PET-LOVER

SHE. I *know* you love me, Richard ... but that's not enough. *(Beat.)* If you really and truly loved me, then you would love Spike, too. *(Indignant:)* He does *not* smell, he is a *very* good dog ... *(Talking "baby talk" to a dog:)* Aren't you a good boy, yes you're Mommy's good boy! *(Back to RICHARD:)* I can't even *believe* you would say such a thing, I hope you haven't damaged his self-image with that brutal, uncaring remark. *(Beat.)* No, no, I don't want you to feel bad, I want you to love Spike. Why is that so difficult? Look at him! *(Gazes worshipfully at the dog.)* Isn't he cute? *(Then, to RICHARD:)* What is wrong with you that you can't love a dog? All he does is offer you unconditional love – and you *shun* him! Well, things are going to change around here. *(Beat.)* What do I *mean*? Well, for one thing, Spikey likes to sleep with me at night – so if we are going to get married, Spike has to be the flower dog. I'm Serious! *And...* remember, you'll have to share the bed with him. *(Beat.)* I am *not* joking. That is not so much to ask, is it? To make room for a dog in your heart ... and your bed? *(Offended:)* He is *not* too big! I mean, yes, he's large, but he's not *enormous*. *(To "SPIKE":)* You're still Mommy's little baby, yes you are! *(To RICHARD:)* I don't want to have to make an ultimatum here, Richard -- "him or me" – but if it comes down to that ... I *will* make one. I will not part with Spike. He holds my heart in his paws every moment of the day ... *(Offended:)* Yes, even when he poops! You are so disgusting sometimes. So what if I made you share his toothbrush? It was only once...and it was supposed to be a bonding experience. Dogs have extremely sanitary mouths, you know. *(An appeal:)* Just let him lick you. Please. Let him lick your ears and you'll see how much love there is in him. *(Offended:)* Honestly! You act as if I'm obsessed with Spike. I'm not obsessed. I'm just a very caring person. *(Fights back tears:)* I mean, maybe this means ... that you and I aren't compatible after all ... I mean, I'm the consummate pet lover and you ... you're a pet-hater!

PET-HATER

HE. I hate pets. I hate their disgusting smells and their filthy, irritating habits ... like peeing on the rug or scratching at fleas all the time – or eating their own feces! *(Shudders.)* It's all so unspeakably vile. That's why I've lived my entire life without the burden of a pet. That is ... until now. *(Sighs.)* You see, after years of misfired dates and thinking there was no hope for me ever being a married man, I finally met the most amazing woman on the planet ... someone I want to share my life with ... So. I propose ... she accepts ... happy ending, right? Wrong. She's a complete pet freak! *(Let me explain:)* She's got this dog named "Spike" ... you'd think she was marrying *him*, not me! She nuzzles him like she's a fellow canine ... she snuggles with him in the bed at night ... she lives her entire life totally planned around this, this beast! *(Beat.)* You may think I'm over-reacting, but I'm not. You have no idea how far she takes it. It's like she's rubbing my nose in it, like she's *testing* me to see how much I can tolerate! *(An example:)* Last night, she insisted that we take him out to dinner with us – which I'm used to by now. Only, on this occasion, I had already planned to pop the question. I started to object to the furry third wheel, but once she started kissing him on the lips, I decided it was best to give in – just to keep things moving. So we get to the restaurant and they have to seat us outside, thanks to Spike. Gone is my pre-arranged romantic corner table, by the fireplace ... gone is the nice, quiet room where I can whisper sweet romantic nothings in her ear ... instead, all that is replaced by the clatter of city busses and the wail of police sirens. And then, just as I'm asking her, "will you marry me?" – Spike starts to hump my leg! She thinks this is all very funny and charming, of course, but it shatters any mood that's been created. I finally take out the engagement ring – and Spike, thinking it's a dog treat, *swallows* it! *(Beat.)* Took five hours for it to come out again, and guess who had to sift through the poop to find it? *(Points to himself.)* Moi. *(Beat.)* At least she washed it off before she put it on. At any rate ... I know that, technically, you folks are only supposed to pick up *stray* animals ... but is there any way the department of animal control could make an exception in this case and rid me of a dog that's an acute threat to the success of my pending marriage?

LITERATE

HE. Oh, no. No, let me put you at ease ... I'm not nearly as "literate" as you might at first presume. What I mean to say is, I'm quite cognizant of my inclusive comprehension of the fundamental basics of our language ... and I usually consider communications skills to be a prerequisite for success in *any* endeavor ... even one such as this. Now, I do hope you're not ... well, *daunted* ... by the fact that I've perused more classic titles than might be found on the shelves of your local library ... and I trust that the Rhodes Scholar status isn't off-putting in any way. Rest assured, in and of itself, that should not stand as a barrier between us. I mean, I can converse as well as any other ordinary denizen in society! *(Beat.)* Talk. I can *talk,* Cynthia. I'm talking now, right? I can be a regular raconteur when I wish to. *(Beat.)* Raconteur, it means someone who is skilled at the art of storytelling. *(Beat.)* All right. Look ... I'll try to simplify it for you: by now, you must realize that I am a genius. My IQ – well, I strive not to *boast* about my IQ – but I can assure you, it is of an extremely high caliber. Moreover, my character is beyond reproach ... and my success in the finance world is unparalleled. *(On the other hand:)* You, my dear, posses no such intellect, skills or faculties. And yet ... you are a gorgeous creature ... and ... well, what I mean to say is – and this is putting the matter fairly clumsily – I am a firm believer in the old adage, "brains and beauty the conqueror make." *(Beat.)* My brains. Your beauty. Don't you comprehend what I'm saying, Cynthia? Together, our union would yield gorgeous, brilliant, invincible offspring! Captains of industry! True, we might not have a tremendous arrange of topics on which to converse, but our children would *become* our topic! *(Beat.)* Cynthia, where are you going? Don't you understand? I am asking you to marry me and bear my offspring!!! *(Beat.)* Look. Just give me a chance. I won't presume to be a Henry Higgins ... rather, perhaps we could try that idea in the opposite direction and you could ... oh, how would one put it ... you could "dumb me down"?

BOOK DUMB

SHE. So there he was, spewin' out all these high-falutin' words ... like I'm *stupid* or somethin' -- I dunno what the hell he's saying. It's like watchin' Egyptian TV or somethin' – blah, blah, blah, these big huge words that don't make no sense at all, gushin' off his tongue like his mouth's a broken water spout. He said he wants me to marry him, if you can believe that! *Marry* him, Celeste! Yeah! *(Beat.)* What do you mean, "that's great?" That *ain't* great! It's awful! It's the most awfulest thing I could ever even imagine, 'cause he's so book-smart and I'm so ... so ... well ... book-*dumb*. I never read one book my whole entire life. Unless, do comic books count? (Beat.) No, I'm not kiddin' you! And the whole time, back in school? I cheated. That's right ... I just skimmed through them *Clint's Notes* or whatever they was. I never read a whole book alla way through to the end and here's Mr. Encyclopedia walkin' around tellin' me that he wants me to have his kids 'cuz I'm so gorgeous! *(Then it hits her:)* I'm gorgeous ... he said that! I'm *gorgeous*! Wow ... I'm gorgeous, Celeste, the smartest guy in this whole friggin' world says so! You shoulda seen him, his eyes was big as hubcaps. *(Beat.)* What am I thinkin'? What do you mean, "what am I thinkin'?" I'm thinkin, who cares if he thinks I ain't smart! He thinks I'm beautiful, and that's more better than ever understandin' all them big words he spews at me! *(Beat.)* So ... if he's so smart and he thinks I'm worth marryin' ... well, I guess I'd really be dumb do say "no"! So what do you say, Celeste? You wanna be my maid of honor?

APPROVAL

HE. It's tough. No matter how hard I've tried to achieve my own goals, they have consistently paled in comparison to his. Every single time. As far back as I can remember, too, it's always been that way. Okay, so maybe my goals weren't as lofty as dad's were ... I mean, right out of high school, I wanted to open a surf shop – while at the same time he set out to challenge the logging industry in the Pacific Northwest. And then there was my friendly neighborhood auto repair shop, which went head-to-head with his bill on making cars more *environmentally*-friendly. *(Shakes his head in weariness:)* You have no idea how hard it has been, being the son of a much-beloved Senator. *(Beat.)* I guess you have your own demons to deal with ... and maybe I set myself up for a fall this time around, too. It's just that ... well, I really thought I had finally created something that he'd be proud of. My own restaurant, a really classy place that the social elite would flock to. Stellar reviews, first-class ratings ... I'm practically the star of the restaurant industry overnight ... and still, he can't bother to stop by and order a salad. *(Beat.)* Serves me right, I guess. I mean, to expect anything from him. All my life, things have been on his terms ... and I suppose they still are. The frustrating thing is, I've really accomplished something pretty significant this time around! I mean, it's amazing, a kid with no education to speak of, I taught myself everything I know and I created this wonderful place ... *(Gestures around him as if in the restaurant.)* But it's not fulfilling at all. So I have to wonder ... maybe a restaurant wasn't my dream at all, huh? Maybe it was really just dad's approval I was seeking. But if that's what I'm really after ... what will happen if I never get it?

LIVING IN THE SHADOWS

SHE. You can't live in a shadow, Eric. *(Beat.)* Well, I think that's exactly what you've been doing: you've been living in dad's shadow for most of your life. *(Beat.)* No, you're right – it's *not* easy for me to say, I certainly fell victim to him myself. *(Thinks back:)* I suppose I thought I had to uphold the reputation of the "Senator's daughter" … whatever that means. *(Beat.)* Well, I don't care what he says, you know how the old man is, what he says and what he means are two different things. Nothing has ever been good enough for him – *nothing* – not even us! His own kids. *(Beat.)* I remember being six years old and making him a paper doll for his birthday … I cut it out all on my own, I colored it, wrapped it up and handed it to him … I guess, even at that young age, I was desperately seeking his approval. And do you know what he said? He snorted and mumbled, "what use would I have with this?" And he threw it away. Threw it away! *(Beat.)* That just broke my heart. I think that's maybe why my gifts to him have grown more extravagant over the years … I've always been trying to buy his love by making my offerings to him more and more impressive. *(Beat.)* But not anymore. Because do you know what I've finally realized, Eric? There's a deficiency all right. But the deficiency is not in me. It's in him. He's the one who's chosen to have a hard heart, he's the one whose chosen to sacrifice his kids' happiness for his own personal ego fulfillment … but we don't have to fall victim to his choices. Or his opinions. You can live your life, free from the grasp of his shadow. I mean, when you really think about it … what can he do to us? Not love us? He's already done that. No matter how much he withholds his love, he can't hurt us. And if you think of him as being a shadow, well, shadows don't have any substance anyway … which means, they can't harm us.

FAIL-SAFE STRATEGY

SHE. Consider yourself lucky, Louise. At least you realized he was a bum before you got stuck with him! Isn't it better to know *now* than when you're having his babies and paying his rent? Anyway, now you have to move on to step number two: cut him loose. *(Beat.)* No, now, listen to me, and listen good. He's got to go! I know it sounds like a daunting task, getting rid of a guy ... but believe me, it *can* be done very quickly and cleanly. I'm gonna share with you my fail-safe strategy for getting rid of unwanted boyfriends. Trust me, I know what I'm talking about. I've used this technique a dozen times before ... and it is guaranteed to drive men away faster than lightning. *(Here's what you do:)* Go to the store and buy a sexy new dress – oh, but be sure'n keep the price tag on so you can take it back the next morning. Then, take a long, relaxing bath and fix yourself up really pretty-like ... make a scrumptious supper like you've never made before ... light some candles ... and then, when he gets to your house, put some really romantic music on ... and start to reel him in, flirt with him, *seduce* him ... and then, when you've got him in the palm of your hand ... ask him to *marry* you. *(Beat.)* I'm serious! I've used it three or four times before and it works like a charm! Of course, Jimmy already had a wife at the time, so he might've been more threatened than most men ... but it triggers a survival instinct deep inside their little brains and they instantly want to escape. Each time I've used this tactic – and it's been at least two or three times ... it's worked perfectly. *(Beat)* Or you could just change your phone number and put a new lock on the door. But then again, some guys are pretty dim. They might not get the hint! This way, you know you're hitting the mark. Asking them to marry you is a fail-safe strategy. If you want to scare a guy away, I totally swear by it! Just put my technique into action...and watch'em run!

VYING FOR VICTORY

SHE. Marco, no! You're not supposed to say "yes!" What's the matter with you, do you *really* think I want to marry you? God, no! I just asked you that because I wanted to *drive you away*! To dump you! Don't you have any common sense?! You're supposed to run screaming from the room! *(Sighs, explains:)* My friend Mary Jean said that all men have this "primitive survival instinct" or something ... and if somebody like me asks you to marry them, you'll turn tail and run! Well, you're not turning tail ... and you're not running! You're – you're sitting! And you're staring. With this pitiful, devoted, "loving" kind of stare ... quit it, Marco! You're grossing me out! And you know me well enough by now to know, I don't like being grossed out! *(An epiphany dawns on her thought:)* Unless ... you're trying to dump *me*. Ah ... that would make sense. Your ego doesn't want to be the one dumped, so you're purposefully doing that worshipful stare so that I'll run off and let you claim the victory! Well, I'm not going to let you win that easily, Marco! I was the one trying to drive *you* away, so go! Be driven! *(Frustrated:)* Ooooh, I told her this wasn't going to be easy! She said this would work, guaranteed, but I knew you were more sophisticated than that! To fall for a simple trick! You're not dumb, Marco, you're smart. Smart and clever and ... oh, my God, what am I doing? You *are* smart! You're a great guy! Only ... you're a worthless bum, aren't you? *(Beat.)* What do you mean, what do I mean, I know for a fact that you haven't had a job in two years, you told me so! I – *(Totally shocked:)* "Independently wealthy?" Oh my goodness ... well ... *(Swallows)* ... do you still want to marry me? *(Brightens:)* You do?! Oh, thank God I listened to Mary Jean. I know this didn't turn out like she *planned* ... but sometimes the best answers are the least expected ones!

MANNERS

SHE. Wash your hands, Leroy. I swear, I wish you'd learn some manners. Honestly. To walk into somebody's house after a lengthy absence and not even bother to wash your hands ... it's a crime. Truly a crime. *(Beat)* And those clothes ... where'd you get that outfit? You look like a referee's corpse that just dug itself out of a grave. And that hair? Who cut it for you, a two-year old child? It looks like it was hacked off with a blunt pocket-knife. *(Beat)* No, Leroy, you listen to me. You come in my house, and you are obliged to show me some respect. And one way of showing respect is to arrive neat, clean and not smelling of sewage. That's the least you could do for a sister you haven't bothered to visit in three years. When did you get paroled, anyway? *(Her mouth drops open in shock.)* What? Oh, my God! Leroy! You're an escaped convict? *(Runs to an imaginary window:)* Did anybody see you come in here? I sure hope not! (Looks back at him:) My goodness, what am I gonna do with you? *(Beat, rolls her eyes:)* No, I am not gonna turn you in! That's the first thing you think of? After all these years? That I'd squeal and drop a dime on you as soon as I laid eyes on you? *(Beat)* Well, that may be true. But the only reason I squealed on you last time and had you sent away is because you were embezzling poppa's money ... and you burned down momma's house ... and killed her dog. I might not have turned you in if it hadn't been for the thing with the dog. But that was heartless, Leroy. Cold and heartless, killing a poor, defenseless ex-show poodle like that. What did that poor dog ever do to you? Huh? Well, just settle down. I'll see if I can rustle up a clean pair of pants and a bowl. *(Beat)* A bowl! To give you a haircut with, stupid, what'd you think? Honestly. Oh, and Leroy? Do us both a favor and take a shower.'Cause if that smell don't evaporate soon... well, that's as good a reason as any to have you hauled off to jail again.

WORTH SOMETHING

HE. *(As if blushing:)* Awww... nobody ever once told me I looked good in prison stripes before. *(On second thought:)* Well, except this one guy in cell block "C"... but I knocked his teeth out. *(Beat)* I'm sorry, that sort of gave you a glimpse of my violent nature ... but y'see, Lorna, when a guy's been put away for a few years like I been, we don't get to see the opposite sex very often. Except on television. And the reception usually ain't that good anyways. I thought Meg Ryan had zits all over her face but come to find out, that was just static on my 13" black and white TV. Anyway, it's been awhile since a female companion's been nice to me ... I just don't quite know how to be nice back. Or ... what to say. It takes awhile to get back into practice. *(Beat)* I guess I could tell you that your hair's pretty ... or that you have a nice smile ... or that your perfume sort of smells like baby puke. *(Beat)* I'm sorry, I can see I upset you, I didn't *mean* to ... my sister says I should just shut my mouth, 'cause nothin' good ever comes out of it. She said she shoulda told on me and sent me back to prison, but she took pity on me and let me slip out of her house unreported. *(Beat)* Look, Lorna, I know I ain't got much to offer you ... I look like a bulldog that chased one too many parked cars and I say stupid things ... and I can't exactly sit down and plan out a life together, seein' as I'm an escaped convict and they might catch me any minute now. But whenever I look at ya, my heart starts beatin' like it might bust right outta my chest. And I don't know if that's love or what ... but it's a mighty powerful feelin' for a guy like me. *(Beat)* If nothin' else, I'm honest, Lorna. That's why I went up the river to begin with, 'cause I wouldn't lie on the stand. Remember when I told you that your perfume smelled like vomit? See, you can always depend on me for the truth. Ain't that worth somethin'? That's gotta be worth somethin'.

THE COUP

SHE. My friend Sophie started a book club. I asked her, I said, "hey, can *I* be a member?" See, Sophie and I go way back. We were in the cheerleading squad together back in high school and she – well, she got married right after college and had those three kids ... or is it four kids now? Anyway, she's the consummate Soccer Mom nowadays and I'm ... well, I'm *not*. She has kids, I don't. I wear dirty, torn sweats to the gym and she shows up in a designer jogging suit. I have a '79 Mazda that leaks oil like crazy and she has a brand new Ford Explorer. Anyway, I heard her over by the Lifecycles talking about her book club with Jenny, who's another Soccer Mom, and I said, "Can I be a member?" At first, she looked at me like I had a giant booger hanging off the end of my nose and said, "you're going to have to *prove* yourself first." And I'm, like, "prove myself?" What the hell is *that* supposed to mean? She mumbled something about me not being very literate, or, I dunno, something like that. I wanted to say, "listen, miss smarty pants, we used to listen to Duran Duran records together, we used to stand out there on the field with short skirts on and shake our booties at football games, you're not the friggin' Poet Laureate of the United States!" But I held my tongue. I said, "okay, when's your next meeting?" And she said, Monday night. So then I went straight to the B. Dalton and I bought a copy of every single *Cliff's Notes* that they had and I locked myself in my condo and I read them all cover to cover, all weekend long. I didn't even stop to eat or pee! By Monday morning, I knew everything there was to know about American Literature. I showed up at the Book Club on Monday night and I blew them all away. *(Beat)* It was really just an acute case of cramming. Like I used to do the night before exams. Of course, back then I usually flunked. But this time, I came through with flying colors! You see, there was a bit of a coup that Monday night ... and the members of the book club elected me as their new president. Which means, Sophie is out in the cold now. Just goes to show you, determination can pay off. *(Beat)* So ... you said you were interested in joining the book club. Could you describe the nine circles of hell outlined in Dante's *Inferno?*

HARPOONED

SHE. Traitor! She's a *traitor*, is what she is! First she comes up to me with this, this *act*, all coy and simple-minded ... "can I join your book club?" She was practically batting her eyelashes! And I fell for it! I let her in and – boom! She harpooned me. *(Beat)* I should've seen it coming. I knew her back in high school and, now that I look back on it, she was always out to sabotage me. She used my favorite Duran Duran album as a Frisbee and put a skip right through *Rio*, which is only their best song! And when we were cheerleaders together, she always ended up at the top of the human pyramid. Always! That's only the most coveted position in a cheerleading lineup, next to squad leader, and she even got picked for squad leader ... *(Thinks back:)* Funny how I got the flu the day they had cheerleader elections ... she always seemed so, so simple ... but even then, she must've been an expert at sabotage! She probably coached Tonya Harding on how to steal the Olympics from Nancy Kerrigan! She's a wolf in sheep's clothing, is what she is, and she's not to be trusted! *(Beat)* Look, Sarah, I know you guys are meeting again this coming Monday ... I'm just wondering if there's any way you could, you know ... stage a revolt. *(Beat)* What do you mean, you "like" her? She's a totally demanding authoritarian! Do you want an authoritarian government? What? "It's just a book club?!" Well, it may *seem* like just a book club ... but it's a *symbol*, Sarah! A symbol of American democracy! You let her get away with this, you might as well hand her the Liberty Bell and a hammer and tell her to crack it the rest of the way! By letting her get away with this, you are letting her shatter the fundamentals of our society! Listen to me! I am not crazy! *(Beat)* All right. Look ... maybe I am getting a little carried away here ... but you know me, Sarah. I'm not one to let go of grudges easily. Either you're with me or you're against me. Either way, I promise you, I will see to it that justice is done.

VAN GOGH LOVE

SHE. Do you love me? I mean, *really* love me? I'm talking a deep, tormented kind of love, a *Van Gogh* kind of love ... like, would you cut off an ear for me? *(Beat)* Or a hand or a foot? It doesn't matter which appendage, I just need a show of commitment, Carl. It's important for me to know, beyond the shadow of a doubt, that you would be willing to take a meat cleaver to some part of your body for me. Because *that* is an example of true love, Carl. The highest example: to suffer bodily harm for your loved one. Van Gogh put it best when he said, "What would life be if we had no courage to attempt anything?" Well, I need to see *your* courage, Carl. I need to feel your courage. I need to *smell* your courage ... and to make sure that it's not spoiled. *Fresh* courage, Carl. I need it fresh, clean and lean. *(Beat)* Now, I don't want you to simply agree because you're afraid of me, Carl. I know that I can be an intimidating person. So was Van Gogh. But if my intimidation scares you away ... well, then, you weren't really all that committed in the first place, were you? And I'm talking about a lifelong commitment, Carl. If we commit to each other, we commit. No turning back. No, "I changed my mind" in ten years. We're playing for keeps here. *(Beat)* So. What'll it be? Ear, nose, finger or toe? You get to choose, Carl. I promise you, I will love you, no matter which appendage you cut off. Because that ... is a Van Gogh kind of love.

SHADOW

HE. My girlfriend's kind of ... well, "clingy's" not the right word ... hmm ... *(He searches for the proper word, then gets it:)* ... *adhesive!* Yeah, she has the kind of devotion that not only sticks to you, it *clings* to you, wherever you go, like a strong scent. Like, if I had to find an analogy in the animal kingdom ... I'd have to say she's like a giant python. *(Wait a minute:)* Is the python the kinda snake that chokes you to death? If that's the one, then she's it. *(Smiles, affectionately:)* My little python ... *(Then, realizes:)* Hey, I'm not saying this like it's a *negative* thing ... I mean, I hope you don't think I'm criticizing her or anything like that. I know, some people might be weirded out by somebody like her, but I happen to like that kind of devotion. She's like the Krazy Glue of relationships, once she takes hold -- whoa! – look out, she's not going *anyplace*! *(Laughs)* Yeah, my life really has changed since I met Karen. She goes with me, everywhere I go. She walks me to work every morning ... waits outside the office building all day long, even in the pouring rain ... and then we walk home together. Some of the guys at work laugh about her, you know, they call her "shadow," they talk about she's always stuck to my side, but growing up alone like I did ... well, there were days when I prayed for somebody like her. Somebody who would never leave me. And I know, unless she gets hit by a Mack truck or something, that Karen will never leave my side. She's there for keeps. She really is my shadow. *(Beat)* There's only one problem ... she's looking for a confirmation of my devotion. She wants me to cut off a finger, or an ear or ... well, it's this kind of a Van Gogh thing. She's really into Van Gogh and thinks I need to show that kind of passion for her. I mean, she believes I'm the one, but she needs *proof* that I'm the one. For me to prove my devotion to her. Does that make sense? Okay ... well, she's going to let me pick the appendage, see ... so which appendage could I lose and not miss it too much? I was figuring on, like, one of my toes, but since I don't type or play any musical instruments, maybe a pinky's the way to go. What do you think?

TEAM PLAYER

HE. Sometimes it's like my head isn't even connected to my body. Like my brain is a helium balloon that's tied to my neck, floating along behind me on a string ... and if somebody were to cut the string – *(Gestures, "it would float away.")* I dunno how to explain it. It's very difficult to keep my brain up with me. Like this morning. I knew I had to get out of the house by eight. So there I was, running around the halls of my apartment at 7:55 like some kind of lab rat, trying to remember everything I'm supposed to have ready. And there comes my brain, two steps behind me. Like a -- what do you call it? – transatlantic phone call, there's a three-second delay. I got my briefcase ... only, I forgot to put any of the case files in it. I grabbed my thermos ... only, I forgot to fill it up with coffee. I managed to take a shower ... only, I forgot to wash my hair. So there I am on the subway with greasy hair, holding a very light briefcase and sucking back air 'cause my thermos is empty ... and I'm thinking, what the hell is the matter with me? And finally my brain catches up with me and I remember, that's right! Some guy named Arturo took a lug wrench and tried to hit a home run with my skull two years ago! *(Beat)* I was voted most promising attorney by the Bar Association, did I ever tell you that? That was before I lost some dopehead's case and he used my head for batting practice one day at the corner of Park and Lex. Nowadays, there are simple tasks that are just ... overwhelming. Believe it or not, standing up in a courtroom and arguing with a judge still comes naturally to me ... all those old cases we studied have somehow stuck in my head ... but weird little things like finding the right courtroom or tying my shoes in the morning, you wouldn't believe how much focus that takes. *(Looks down.)* Yes, that's why I bought loafers. My whole closet is now filled with loafers. Back before Arturo, I wouldn't have been caught *dead* in loafers, but now ... *(Beat)* Be patient with me, Fred. You know I'm a team player. I may not be your strongest team player, but I promise you, I'll play for all I'm worth. You can count on it.

THE THIRD ARM

HE. I used to know this guy who had a third arm. *(Beat)* Yeah, *literally* a third arm, sticking out of his side. Or maybe it was his back, I can't remember, I was only a kid at the time. His same was "Sully" – or at least that's what the kids in the neighborhood called him. He wore these really bulky sweatshirts all the time to hide his deformity from everyone. In around third grade, Sully became an entrepreneur of sorts. See, he would charge the other kids a dime to see his third arm on the playground. One day, some fifth graders beat him up and took all his money and kept yelling at him, "why don't you fight back, Sully? You got three arms and we only got two!" But Sully took the beating. A few days later, he disappeared from school altogether. I heard he had the arm amputated, and years later, at our high school reunion, somebody said that Sully, whose passion if you can believe it was baseball, even played in the minors. *(Beat)* I know, I know you don't follow me. I'm just taking a trip down memory lane here, but it's leading me someplace ... you see, I've got what you might call a moral dilemma. Or is it ethical? What's the difference between a moral dilemma and an ethical dilemma? Anyway, I got a third arm, so to speak, on *my* team. Useless. Only, we keep it around because we're – what? Sentimental? I dunno. But I think maybe it's time to cut it loose. *(Beat)* Tom. I'm talking about Tom. Guy who got it with the baseball bat to the head a few years ago? Yeah, he's bright. But only in certain areas. He can't tie his shoes and he can barely write his name – but he can wrangle with a judge for hours on end. Still, a team's only as strong as its weakest member, right? And this guy ... he ain't the strongest. I think it's time to cut him loose. Unless you can give me a good reason to keep him. So what's it gonna be, Marty? Amputate ... or save the limb?

FOIBLES

HE. What do you mean, I'm looking at you "funny?" I'm *not* looking at you funny! I'm looking at you the way I *always* look at you ... which is *not funny*! *(Beat)* No, no, no ... we are *not* arguing, arguing is when you throw things at each other and curse and blurt out stuff you'll regret later. I'm not throwing or cursing or blurting ... I'm just pointing out that you might want to reconsider your choice, that's all. No, I'm *not* judging you or criticizing you, I'm just "pointing out." That's my job as your new husband, isn't it? To point things out. Like ... your foibles. *(On second thought:)* – ah, not that you *have* any foibles, I just mean, it's my job to point things out in general. *(Beat, then a sigh:)* I don't know what to say, Delores, you told me you wanted to buy the lampshades, I asked you, "are you *sure*?" I was just trying to make sure that *you* were sure! That's all I was doing. *(Beat)* Because! It's like bringing a pet into the home ... adopting a child ... buying home furnishings requires the same consideration. The same careful concern. The same thought process. After all, we might be living the rest of our lives with these lamps towering over us ... shining down on us ... we want to make sure they're the right ones. *(Big sigh, then:)* Okay. All right. I confess. I think they're hideous. I think they're the ugliest things on this whole entire planet but I didn't want to tell you that because I didn't want to hurt your feelings. I wanted to avoid a fight at all cost, but *I DESPISE THEM!* I know they would give me nightmares! I would rather hang a bare bulb from the ceiling than light our room with those gaudy, ugly things!!! *(Beat)* What? You *agree*? Thank God, Delores. I'm so glad we share the same tastes ... I'd hate to start things off with a big fight.

CONTROL FREAK

SHE. Ugh! You are *such* a little weasel ... I can't stand it anymore! I know we've only been married for – *(Checks watch.)* – eighteen hours, but you're driving me up the wall! *(Realization dawns:)* I see now! I do! I see what's been going on ... you're a *control freak*! No, don't interrupt me, I'm piecing it all together now ... *(Thinks back:)* It all makes sense all of a sudden, all your little "behaviors" ... like, like ... always getting my coffee for me. I always say, "two sugars," and you always put in *one*. Why? Because you want to make mine be like yours! Like the way *you* like it. *(Realization:)* I see now ... the whole time we were dating, you completely controlled everything I said, thought or did! Don't deny it! What about the time I bought that dress for the holiday office party? You cleverly arranged for Stacy's Chihuahua to wee-wee all over it just moments before the party so that I'd be forced to wear the one *you* liked! How'd you pull that off anyway, huh? Did you make that little lapdog drink water all day? *(Beat)* Yeah, well, I'm onto you now, Richard. I know we're only newlyweds, but I make up half of us and I want you to know, I am *through* being controlled! I have my own opinion, thank you very much, and I am going to voice it! To shout it loud and clear from the top of the highest mountain! I am my own woman. I have my own wants, needs, desires and opinions, and -- *(Beat)* What? The lampshades? Well, I think ... I think ... *(Beat)* Gee, I don't know, what do *you* think?

COLLATERAL DAMAGE

HE. *(Tough Mafia guy:)* Do we have to go through this *again*? It's really not that hard to comprehend. She asked me, "can I borrow a cup of milk?" ... So I shot her. *(Beat)* You gotta understand, a guy in my position ... *(Looks around, lowers voice:)* A guy in my position is *always* faced with some element of risk, some degree of suspicion. You might call it paranoia, but I call it bein' careful. I took a huge risk, getting up there in Federal Court and telling what all I knew. How many death threats did I get back then, huh? Yeah, we lost count! So it's only natural to walk around, thinking that somebody's always watching over your shoulder, somebody's always following your every move ... or at least, that's how it feels. You tend to get a little jumpy after awhile. Like, at any moment, I might be doin' the laundry or lightin' the barbecue grill ... and BLAM! -- all of a sudden, I might get it right in the back of the head. Plus, I've had a bit of a rough spell lately, hearin' about Joey Carmello and Ricky "Elbows" getting whacked out in wherever they were. "Witness Protection." Hah. Some *protection* ... *(Beat)* No offense. It's just that, this broad rings the doorbell at, what? Five o'clock in the morning? Okay, *eight* ... and wakes me up, askin' to borrow a cup of milk. So, what am I supposed to do? Huh? Have you looked inside my fridge? Just in case you haven't noticed, I don't *do* milk! So, there she is at the door and instantly my brain is goin' in nine thousand different directions: is she for real, is the whole "milk thing" an act, it seems too innocent to be real, is there a shooter in the car out there ...? And so on. *(Beat)* She shouldn't've reached for her measuring cup. If she hadn't a done that ... she might still be alive. But I saw that movement and -- BOOM. Down she goes. *(Beat)* It was an accident, okay? And she was just what you might call ... collateral damage.

MODERN-DAY HOUDINI

SHE. *(Tough Federal Marshall:)* All right, Murph, you listen to me, and you listen good. You can't just keep *mowing down* everybody who spooks you! *(Beat)* No, no, I *know* ... you claim women don't "spook" you. You're a real tough cookie, Murph. But the truth is, some poor lady showed up at your front door and you blew her away! *(Beat)* She was a *civilian*, Murph! She had nothing to do with anything! She just had the horrible misfortune of ringing your doorbell at precisely the wrong moment and waking you up ... and now *my* life is a living hell because of it! *(Beat)* Because, Murph. *I'm* the one who has to clean up the mess. I'm the one who's on call 24-7, I have to be like some covert, modern-day Houdini in spike heels and a skirt. It's my job to erase all the traces ... to make it seem like she never even existed! Do you know how hard that is? To go through my day, wondering if, at any moment, my phone might ring and I'll find out that you've flipped your lid again? *(Beat)* I know. I know you did the right thing eighteen months ago in Federal Court. You came forward and a whole bunch of scumbags got put away for a long, long time. I know all that. But remember this, Murph: you're only as safe as I am thorough. In other words, you'd better not tick me off ... or some of your "mistakes" might just catch up with you. Capiche?

THE VULTURESS

SHE. You wouldn't *believe* my boss! She asked me to account for where I *am* all day! Ugh! This is so Draconian, so Totalitarian! This whole place has turned into a dictatorship before our very eyes! The Evil Vulturess said if I can't account for where I am all day, I'm fired! *(Beat)* Oh! Good idea. We'll write it all out, then I can show her ... *(Gets out paper and pencil.)* Okay. Well, let's see ... well, I usually get in around nine ... then I go to the ladies' room 'til 9:45 ... you know, to freshen up for the day ... then I get coffee ... and I'm back at my desk around 10:30. *(Beat)* What? Oh, well, from 9:45 to 10:30 is getting coffee time. You know, catching up on things with the other secretaries ... then from 10:30 to 11:00 is answering e-mail time. Oy, I despise spammers. Always sending me those awful sex things and offers for Viagra. *(Beat)* No, I know the Company filters those out, I'm talking about my *personal* e-mail! *(Continuing:)* Then at 11:30 I go to lunch ... and it's only occasional – *very* occasional – that I go shopping, in which case I am back at my desk by 2:15. On most days, I'm back at my desk by 2:00 sharp. Then, for the whole entire rest of the day, I work like I'm in some kind of chain gang! *(Beat)* Well, except for my afternoon coffee break, which is from 3:00 to 3:45 – that's required by law, y'know. Then, from around 4:00 to 4:30, I split my spleen open for this wretched place and, at 4:45, I gather my things up to go home. *(Looks over the list and smiles:)* There, now. We've figured it all out! I've accounted for the whole entire day! Wow ... The Vulturess is really gonna be eatin' some crow *now,* doncha think?

COMPROMISING SITUATION

SHE. She calls me "The Vulturess." *(Beat)* Do you have any *idea* how it feels to be nicknamed after a carnivorous bird of prey? A bird that feeds on carrion? It's offensive, that's what it is, and I've grown weary of it. There have been too many insults, too many sideways glances, far too much sloth on her part ... and now, that girl has got to go. *(Beat)* I *realize* it's difficult to fire someone these days, Wembley, I'm not stupid. I didn't get this high up the corporate ladder by being ignorant. *(Plotting:)* No, I've got to arrange some sort of compromising situation for her. *(Sighs; apparently "Wembley" doesn't follow.)* Do I have to be *literal* here? Honestly, you're so dim sometimes, Wembley ... *(The pitch:)* What if she were to steal some office supplies? Some pads of paper in her purse? A calculator in her carry-all? *(Another idea:) Or* ... she's always checking her insipid e-mail account ... what if she were to send corporate secrets over the Internet? She's always leaving her keyboard unattended, wandering off to God knows where ... what if ... *(Looks at "Wembley" with meaning:) someone* ... were simply to type in some incriminating information and click "send"? Oh, it would need to happen more than once. Say, over a period of weeks ... then I could have Information Services audit her account and – presto! She has no way to disprove it. *(Smiling)* Perhaps I *am* evil, Wembley ... but I'd rather be evil and successful than stupid and unemployed. Wouldn't you agree?

LIFE IS A RIVER

HE. John, listen to me. I know I'm going to sound insensitive here ... but you've got to find some way to put it behind you. *(Beat)* No, don't go, don't – hear me out, John. Please! Just hear me out. It's the least you can do for me. For your only brother. *(Pause)* I've never said this to anybody before ... but all my life I've envied you. Envied your career ... your accomplishments ... Barbara ... and then little Leanne. I've watched from afar as the two of you raised her, loved her ... and then lost her. My heart aches too, John, believe me. I love her as well. I love *all* of you, that's why I'm telling you this. You've beat yourself senseless with blame and self-loathing. I know, I know – you made a mistake and she was taken from you – and for all we know, you'll never see her again. You should've been watching her and you got wrapped up in something else and the next thing you knew, she was gone – taken – but – John, no, John, wait – let me finish. *(Beat)* Life is a river, John, and it keeps flowing. But you ... you're stuck on the bank watching it go by. You've already lost Leanne and you'll lose Barbara too, if you don't change the way you're thinking. You've got to forgive yourself, John. That's your only way out. You've got to find it in you to forgive yourself and move on. There's still a life to be lived ... a good, long life ... *(Beat)* I want to be able to envy you again. I know I can't imagine what it's been like ... but I can imagine what it *could* be like ... and I want you to be able to do that. To *imagine* again. It's time to start, John. And I just want you to know ... I'm here to help you.

SINGLE STRAY MOMENT

HE. No, you *can't* imagine what it's like. There's no way. *I* never could've imagined it, either, never could have comprehended such grief ... such complete, total, all-consuming grief. *(Pause)* That grief is always inside me, every moment of every day ... it's stuck in my throat when I wake up in the morning and it grips my heart with every beat. *(Beat)* Sleep? That doesn't help. In some ways, that's even worse. That's when your mind is free to roam, to imagine what might be ... or what might have been ... you see, when you sleep, it's your dreams that are the target. Your dreams become filled with horrible, torturous images of smiling faces ... outstretched arms ... childlike laughter ... *(Pause)* Perhaps if we knew for certain ... if we had some *confirmation* ... if we could be convinced that she were dead ... well, then, maybe we could mourn her. Close that chapter and move on. But we can't mourn her, because we don't know where she is or what's happened to her. And as a result, we're stuck in this awful chasm somewhere between mourning and hope ... between grief and expectation. That at some moment, the phone will ring and the authorities will tell us that they've found her. *(Beat)* Would she even remember us? It's been so long ... and the worse part of it all is, you keep reliving that one moment. That single stray moment when you took your eyes off her – just for a split second – and she disappeared into the crowd. A little four year old, swallowed up in the moving sea of people on a busy street ... her precious little face disappearing beneath an army of umbrellas on a rainy September day ... and then gone forever. But not really gone, is she? Because I see her again and again and again ... every time I close my eyes. *(Pause)* You're right. You don't know what it's like. And I hope you never do.

DECLARATION OF INDIVIDUALITY

SHE. I am so sick and tired of everybody telling me what to do! And you – *you're* the worst offender of all! No matter what I say, no matter what I *think*, you're all over me with a million and one reasons for why *I'm* wrong and why I'm destined to end up a failure! But I'm not gonna be the failure, Mom. Your whole point of view of me is colored because of how things turned out for *you*. In case you haven't notice, *you're* the failure! *(Beat, catches herself.)* I'm sorry ... I don't really mean that ... it's just, whenever you talk about "when you were my age" and all the possibilities that you had ... where you were headed with your life ... I dunno, I just look at you now, and it's, like, what *happened*? You had so much going for you and you totally blew it. I'm gonna move out sooner or later – hopefully sooner – and you'll be stuck all alone in this dumpy trailer. *(Rolls eyes.)* I'm sorry, "manufactured home." God, Mom, will you give it a rest? Everybody knows this is a trailer park. True, it's Santa Monica, but still ... *(Beat)* And you *never* talk about Dad. It's like I *have* no father, he's just this huge black hole that you will never acknowledge and I ask you about him and I get nothing! I'll bet you drove him away too, didn't you? Just like you're doing with me! *(Beat)* No, Mom, this time it's *my* turn. I'll stay here for six more months, I have to, I know that. But then I'll be old enough to make my own choices, and you'd better believe I am ready to make them. I'm not your little girl anymore, in case you haven't noticed, my room is no longer pink, it is black. That was my declaration of individuality and you can't stop me from being who I am! It's inevitable, Mom. You just have to accept it.

BAD BLOOD

SHE. Was I wrong, Jenny? To put her first, I mean. Sometimes I wonder ... *(Beat)* I mean, it seemed like the right choice at the time. Oh, what am I saying? It's seemed like the right choice all along! It sure wasn't easy, but I wasn't looking for easy, I was looking for what was right. And you know me. When I commit to something, I totally commit. All these years, I have tried to never look back. I checked my wants and needs at the door sixteen years ago and embraced motherhood with all that was in me. *(Beat)* But now things are changing. You know what I'm talking about, it happened with your girls. My darling nieces ... only, I guess it wasn't quite as traumatic in your household. Or maybe everything's just amplified in a trailer. *(Catches herself.)* "*Manufactured* home." Yes, that's what I always call it, isn't it? *(Beat)* I didn't have a choice, Jenny. She didn't have a father. How could I let her grow up without a mom, too? When you get right down to it, I'm all she's got in this world. *(Beat)* She'll realize that. One of these days, she'll know that and, whatever bad blood is between us ... she'll come home. The hard part is picking up the pieces and putting the broken cookie jar back together. Figuring out who "I" am again. I used to have such a clear sense of myself and now ... *(Shrugs)* Is it like riding a bicycle after a long time? You know, you haven't done it for years but somehow it all comes back? I sure hope so. Because I'm so far away from that part of me ... I worry that I'll never find it again.

I KNOW HOW TO GET EVEN

SHE. Hey, you don't want to cross me. *Ever.* 'Cause believe you me, I *know* how to get even. *(An example:)* Last year, Richard began pointing out to me – *usually* in front of my friends – that I had gained some weight. Duh! Like I *needed* to be reminded! During the course of the summer alone, I must've heard every juvenile fat joke in the book. You know, "what do you call a life-sized bowl of flesh-colored Jell-O? My *wife.*" Yeah ... So I went to Sears one afternoon on my lunch break and bought myself a brand-new, top of the line Singer sewing machine. *(Beat)* Oh, no, not to let my clothes *out* ... to take his *in.* One centimeter at a time. It was really amazing. You see, he barely even noticed it at first. By Day 7, he had started to look preoccupied a lot of the time. Then, around Day 15, his endless torrent of "fat jokes" suddenly stopped. But *I* didn't stop ... I kept taking those trousers in until he limped whenever he walked. He went out and bought some new ones. And I took them in, too. I went to a carnival warehouse and bought a "fat mirror" that I installed in the visor of his car. I re-calibrated the bathroom scale so that even though it read "0" when he got on, there were ten extra pounds on it! As the days went on, I saw Richard crumble before my very eyes. He had started out as a tyrant and soon became a beaten man. *(Beat) Now*? Well, we're up to Day 44. I think maybe it's time to break the news to him. This morning he said something about a starvation diet. Not for *me* ... for himself. So I guess I made my point.

ALLIANCE

SHE. Ginny? Do you have a moment? Hi, my name's Charlene. I work up on the third floor? Yeah, well, I heard you were *(Whispers:) an expert* ... at getting revenge. *(Beat)* That whole story about what you did to your husband? Wow, that was brilliant. And, because of that, well, you're sort of a legend in the file room. Anyway, what I was wondering, was, I was wondering if I could maybe, you know... *hire* you to help me get revenge on my boss. Mr. Shepansky. Yeah, the one with the full head of hair, right. *(Beat)* Do I have a plan? Well, I *did*...but here's the problem: when he went down to the company gym last week, I took his keys and went out and made copies of them all. Then I waited until he was away at that weekend symposium with his wife and I let myself into his house. I snuck into his bathroom and I put some Nair – just a little bit – in his shampoo. I let myself out again, careful not to leave any traces. Then I – *(Looks around, as if someone is passing by within earshot, then lowers voice:)* – then I *waited*. But nothing happened. His hair stayed just as full and shiny as ever. Days passed ... but it didn't appear to be working. Then his wife dropped by, and I couldn't believe it ... her hair had thinned and I could see her scalp! See, it was *her* shampoo! I didn't mean to make her lose *her* hair, she's the nicest woman on the planet. Anyway, he started acting coldly towards her and calling her, "baldy." *(Beat)* Well, at first I wanted to get revenge on him because he was a bum to *me*, but now he's being a bum to her, too! So I confided in her what I'd done. And she *loved* it! Seems he's been a jerk to her for years now. So ... she and I have formed an alliance ... and we want to hit him. Hard. Do you have any suggestions? We're willing to pay top dollar for any scheme you can cook up. This is war. Shepansky is the enemy ... and we're not taking any prisoners.

LINES IN THE SAND

SHE. What do you want me to say? I don't care that I hurt their feelings! And there is *no way* he's going over there again. Ever! *(Points offstage, softening:)* Look at him, playing out there ... eight years old and he's telling *me* how to load a *gun*?! *(Beat)* You know how hard it's been. We have tried against all odds to raise Nathan in a very innocent environment. We wanted to let him be a child as long as we could. There's such a rush these days for kids to grow up, what's wrong with having a childhood? I dunno about you, but I enjoyed that time when I was little. These days, it seems like it's sacrificed so early, at such a young age. *(Beat)* You know me. I have always screened his friends carefully. There was that one family, the – oh, the Mathisons. I used to let him go over there and play with them, but when he came home saying *you know what* at the dinner table, that was the end of that. But compared to this, that was *nothing*! I mean, hey – "bathroom words" should be my biggest fear, right? *(Here it is:)* He came home last week and he was explaining to me how to load a gun. I just assumed they were playing with toys over there, at which point I'm about to have a meltdown anyway, 'cause you know how I feel about *toy* guns! *(Beat)* So I called her. Yes! I got her on the phone and I said, I don't appreciate your exposing my child to toy guns. And she said, "oh, no, you're wrong. *They weren't toys*!" Yes! And "not to worry, we were supervising it all very carefully. Dave was just showing off his gun collection to the boys." So matter of fact, like that's what you do with every eight-year-old boy who comes over to the house! *(Beat)* Well, I don't care what anybody says, it's over. He is not going over there again. I don't care how many lines I have to draw in the sand ... I vow to protect his innocence as long as I can.

CRYING WOLF

HE. Who the hell does she think she *is*? Correct me if I'm wrong, but if this is still the United States, I can own a gun if I want to. Right? Long as I don't go out there and shoot anybody – and you *know* I'd never shoot anybody! – in which case, it's entirely *my* business – our business. *(Rolls his eyes:)* "Endangering the kids" ... we never endangered *anybody*! I just showed those boys how to clean a shotgun. Pointed out where the shells go ... it's not like I drove 'em out to the shooting range and invited them to join me in target practice! I wish you'd just hung up on her. *(Beat)* Yeah, well, I'm sure *she's* perfect, huh? She's never done anything wrong in her whole entire life, so she's free and clear to cast stones at me! *(Beat)* No, I am not blowing this up into a full-scale fracas, she's the one who started it all! Ran to the PTA and stirred 'em all up, they think I'm practically a murderer by now! *(Suddenly taken aback.) What* did you say? Me apologize? For *what*? I'm not gonna apologize to anybody! What have *I* got to apologize for? That I have a different system of values than this woman? Than her rich, fancy friends? I grew up in a house with guns and so did my father, did anybody get shot and killed? Did any of us grow up to be felons? Are there any injured or maimed cousins lying in the graveyard because we had guns in the house? No! *(Beat)* Look, I am going to stand on my principles. My principles are time-honored ... and, at the end of the day, we'll see who was right and who was just cryin' wolf. *(Beat)* See, the thing is ... the thing about cryin' wolf ... if a *real* wolf shows up at the door, what are you gonna do? You gotta be able to shoot him. It's the only way to truly defend yourself.

DON'T TALK WITH YOUR MOUTH FULL

HE. I can still hear you and Dad telling me, "don't talk with your mouth full!" I never did get it. I was six years old, y'know, so I always thought, what's so *horrible* about describing my day at Kindergarten with a mouth full of saltines? Okay, so you guys catch a glimpse of a few chewed-up crackers, big deal! *(Beat)* Well, it took me twenty years, but I think I finally may have learned my lesson, Mom. Y'see, I had this big job interview last week. I was up for a gig at this really prestigious firm. Actually, it was my third interview with them, I had aced the first two and now I was in the final stretch. I was meeting the head honcho for lunch at the nicest restaurant in town – the kind of place you have to wait *three months* to get into. So we sit down to two plates of high-class rabbit food and a gourmet caviar sampler ... and the big guy asks me, "so, what line of work is your father in?" I had just bitten into this huge slice of cheese toast and I said, "trucking." 'Cuz my Dad's a trucker. But ... with a mouth full of food, it didn't sound like "trucking." It sounded infinitely *worse*. Yeah, you see where this is headed. The guy's eyes got so wide, he almost choked! I reached for my glass of water – but I'd already drank it. So I tried to say, "Lord, no" – but it must've sounded like "porno," 'cause he got even more upset! He was turning red and his veins were standing out on his head now! I stood up to save myself but I realized that I'd spilled a dollop of caviar on my lap, so as I reached down to brush it off, I yelled, "let me start over!" – but it came out like, "let me show you!" He fell out of his chair and ran out of the place. He never even looked back. *(Beat)* The worst part of it all was, I got stuck with the check. $80 wroth of caviar and stale bread. And Joannie is absolutely furious at me, she's the one who got me the interview in the first place. But I told her, just like I'm telling you ... at least I learned my lesson. Surely that's worth the loss of a job and an $80 lunch tab, don't you agree?

BARBARIAN

SHE. I swear, sometimes my fiancée is such a barbarian! "Cro-Magnon" might be the more appropriate term. His favorite impulses seem to be eating, making out and sleeping. Honestly. He blew this entire job interview that I set up for him, just because he crammed his mouth full of food during a luncheon meeting and spit out nonsense, his cheeks bulging like a chipmunk. He swears he's learned his lesson, but that was merely the lesson on eating with his mouth full. There are so many *more* "lessons" he has yet to learn, and I'm tired of playing teacher! *(Beat)* Well, like the *staring thing* ... you see, he's the consummate "people watcher." Which is all well and good, but what that *literally* means is that he stares at people whenever we're in public! *(For example:)* There was this couple having a fight on the subway the other day – an argument, I should say, this man and a woman. A very heated argument. Now, most people, respecting the couple's privacy, would look away. That's what I did. That's what everyone else on the *train* did. But not Desmond. He kept staring at them, watching them ... like he was mesmerized. I gave him a solid elbow to the ribs and whispered, "this *isn't* Reality TV." But he couldn't take his eyes off them. The man finally looked up and saw Desmond watching and called out, "what's *your* problem?!" I was afraid that he was going to beat Desmond to a pulp right then and there -- but luckily we arrived at our stop and got off before any blood was shed. *(Beat)* Another thing that I deplore is his constant "adopting" of other people's ideas. Let him listen to half an hour of Rush Limbaugh and he's a staunch right-winger ... then hand him section one of the *LA Times* and, by the time he's through, he's a Liberal. *(Beat)* I thought Desmond was so ... *deep* ... at first, but now I realize that "deep" and "vacant" walk a close line together. It's just too bad he's so cute. That's what raises this whole issue from an irritation ... to a dilemma.

SITTING DUCK

HE. *(With a backwoods drawl:)* Let's go over this one more time, Wilbur. *Our* job is to shoot the guns, *your* job is to run and duck. *(Beat)* Duck – you know. *(Demonstrates, then listens and reacts:)* Darn right I'm serious! What did you think you were in for when you signed up for "target practice"? *You're* the target! Now, now, don't go gettin' all squeamish on me, Wilbur. Amos and me are good shots. Well, *I* am, anyway. Amos is utmostly reliable when he's sober ... *(Looks over an imaginary "Amos")* ... are you sober, Amos? *(Shrugs)* Oh, well. At least you can count on *me*. That is, unless'n my glass eye comes loose again. See, we ain't got a whole lot of "entertainment" up here in the hills. Not like you back in the city. You got car accidents, muggings, natural disasters ... all we got is huntin'. You didn't know all this when you signed up for "target practice" at that general store, did ya? Nobody ever does ... *(Down to the instructions:)* Okay, now. Here's how this is gonna go: when the dogs bark, you start running, lickety-split. *(Laughs)* Why? Cause if'n ya don't, we'll *shoot* ya! That's the whole point! See, you got to run through the pig pen, around the barn, underneath that tractor and dive into the pond. *(Beat)* Right. The one with the dead horse in it. If you can swim the length of that pond and crawl out at the other end – through the rusty barb wire – and make your way through the corral full of pit bulls, then you win! I figure you've got at least a 80-20 chance. That's 80 in favor of serious maiming. So ... that was my pep talk. You ready for us to untie you and set you to runnin', or do you need to do some "warm-ups" first? Okay ... untie him, Amos! *(Pause)* All right ... on your mark ... get set ... wait. *(Reaches up to his eye:)* My glass eye's come loose. Ah ... tell ya what: let's take five and we'll try this again. What do you say, Wilbur?

GRAND PATTERN

SHE. Wilbur, you are *such* a bad liar! I swear ... *(Beat)* What, are you *kidding*? Do you *really* expect me to believe that you missed our rehearsal dinner because of that lame, ridiculous story you cooked up? *(Beat)* Because! Hillbillies don't kidnap normal people and drag them off into the woods and use them for target practice! And don't show me those marks again, *anybody* could put scratches on their wrists like that and claim they were rope burns. Honestly, tied-up by a family of bucktoothed, gun-toting rednecks? That's insane! *(Beat)* Oh, and what *really* put me over the edge, by the way, was that absurd notion about the glass eye. *Nobody* has glass eyeballs, not in this day and age! Haven't you ever heard of eye transplants? *(Beat)* All right, then explain this to me: how could he aim his gun if he had glass eyes? No, *you* said – arrgh! I can't even believe I'm *debating* this! The point is, now I see that this is all part of a pattern. A grand pattern on *your* part to purposefully sabotage our wedding. No, let me finish!*(Beat)* You've been very subtle, I'll give you that ... I might even go so far as to say passive aggressive ... but now that I look back, ever since we set the date, you seemed to be more distracted than usual. I didn't want to admit it to myself, I guess I just wanted to chalk it up to the fact that you were simply preoccupied with other things ... but now I see. I see a grand pattern that's formed: you "forgetting" to tell everybody at work that we were getting married ... you "not being able" to find your birth certificate ... you "not understanding" what day we were supposed to meet with the minister ... and now *this*? You miss our one and only rehearsal dinner because you were supposedly dragged into a real-life version of "Deliverance," minus Ned Beatty? Enough, Wilbur! This is it! The buck stops here. You have to prove to me that you *really* want to get married, once and for all or we're through! And this time I mean it!

THOUGHT CHAMELEON

HE. A great man once said, "knowledge is power." *(Beat)* You're a smart fellow, Isaac. Do *you* feel powerful? *(Laughs, then sighs and continues:)* I must admit, for most of my own life, I've been a fairly ignorant person. I'd never taken the time – or, *had* the time, rather – to *learn* about current affairs ... world events ... local politics ... but then something happened one day that proved to be a Godsend – and, in essence, it was the very key to my success. *Eavesdropping. (Beat)* It all started when I was sitting in that coffee shop over on Main Street – Earl's, you know the place – and I overheard Bill McCutchen saying, "there's no way Jimmy would win the Alderman race if folks find out he's embezzling." He was talking about Jim Zimmer, who, as it turned out, *did* embezzle about $12,000 from one of his clients. *(Beat)* What? How do *I* know? Because! I snuck into his office that night and went through his files! What's more, I'm the one who *leaked* the files to the newspaper and blew his campaign out of the water. And who won in his place? Moi. The point is, ever since that morning in Earl's, I've made a habit out of eavesdropping ... finding out what other people think ... and using their opinions as my own. I like to think of myself as a "thought chameleon." My wife calls me "a spineless fool without any ideas in his head." *(Smiles)* But she doesn't mind the thought of living in the Governor's mansion ...*(Leans forward, conspiratorially:)* And that's why we're here today, Isaac. I won the Alderman race ... and the Mayor's race ... all on my own, despite one unfortunate bit of misinformation that almost sidetracked me. But I'm going to need a little help to get to the State Capital. Now, a little bird told me that you have the inside scoop on the Governor's infidelities. Don't turn away, Isaac. You see, I've heard a few stories about *you* as well. And once I share them with you ... well, I'm sure you'll want me to keep them quiet. Get my drift?

ALL EARS

SHE. I'd be extremely careful if I were you, Daniel. After all, you shouldn't trust everything that comes out of *my* mouth. I mean, for all you know, everything I'm telling you is lies. *(Beat)* What I mean is ... well, it all started with that creep Bob Wintergreen ... he was always *listening* to me. Like some kind of "sound byte leech," always hanging around, following me, hoping to "overhear" some dirt on somebody in City Hall. *(Beat, then a smile creeps over her face:)* But I sure showed *him*. Mm-hmm, I finally realized that the things I was whispering in the coffee shop or sharing in the mall with my friends were turning up in the newspaper. Things about my boss! And when things are being leaked about the *Mayor* ... well, his aides start sniffing around to find out who the culprit is. It wasn't intentional or anything, you know, a little anecdote told to a girlfriend, a funny story shared with a date ... but eventually I put two and two together and got Bob. You see, Bob Wintergreen was making campaign speeches that echoed personal tidbits about the Mayor. Tidbits *I'd* shared with friends and colleagues. And, being the executive secretary, I'm one of the very few who has access to this kind of information. So I decided to test my theory ... I met Rhonda at Earl's Coffee Shop one day ... and I made sure to take an empty table in the corner. Sure enough, here comes Bob Wintergreen, taking a seat right behind me. So I started my own "unofficial" misinformation campaign, right there at Earl's! I laid out the most ludicrous story imaginable ... about the Mayor's bid to raise parking meter fees from 25 cents to five dollars. But I did it with complete conviction. The result? He fell for it, hook, line and sinker. The next day, he came out with this ridiculous movement to "repeal the parking meter scandal." Of course, there was no scandal, but from that point on, I knew whom to avoid. *(Beat)* The reason I'm telling you all this is, I think Bob Wintergreen has ears in *your* office – the Governor's office. You've got to watch this guy, Daniel, he's all ears, he can hear through walls practically! I'm afraid he may have gotten to one of your co-workers. So be careful whom you trust. And be *very* careful about what you say. Your next words could be the last ones you speak ... in the Governor's mansion.

IMMORTALITY

HE. I think you've missed the whole point. *Yes*, we threw a surprise party for him ... but the goal wasn't to make him happy ... it was to *kill* him! *(Beat)* Look, the man is 97 years old. 97 years old and not even a *hint* of his slowing down. He's just as mean and ornery as he was half a century ago! How many of his heirs has he screwed over in the past five decades? Hmm? You wanna guess? I'll tell you: *all* of 'em. That's right, in one way or another, old man Phinneas scorned, alienated, dumped on or mistreated *everybody* in this family! He's filthy rich ... but he doesn't share his wealth with *anybody* – blood relatives included. *(A couple of examples:)* I got fired from the ad agency three years ago. I interviewed for months but couldn't seem to nail down another job. Finally, I got one, but it didn't start for, like, eight weeks or something. And unless I made a mortgage payment right then, I was going to lose the condo. So I asked him for a loan. A *loan* – not a gift! Well, you would've thought I'd asked him for his own blood the way he tore into me. And of course, you know the rest of the story – I got foreclosed on. I *still* haven't straightened my credit out. And it wasn't like I was some distant relative, I'm his grandson! *(Beat)* Then there was Uncle Herbert and the surgery incident. Poor Herbie didn't have any insurance, so he went to the old man and asked for some help – otherwise he couldn't afford to have his bypass. The old man just sneered and said, "*real* men don't worry about their cholesterol, real men just eat lots of red meat and die when their time comes." Uncle Herbert dropped dead six months later. Aunt Esther still won't forgive the old man for that. So you can see, in one way or another, we *all* have reason to hate him. So we thought – *assumed*, anyway – that if we triggered a big, elaborate surprise party, he'd be so shocked that he'd have a heart attack and drop dead right on the spot! But did he do what we wanted? No, of *course* not! Once again, he fooled us all. It's like he read our minds, he knew exactly what we were up to and vowed he'd outlive us all before he'd die and leave us any of his money. *(Beat)* I never believed in immortality ... but now I'm starting to think that the old man is going to live forever.

HEARTLESS

SHE. How can you be so heartless? I'm not asking you for a handout, I'm asking you for a *hand*. Why is that so difficult for you? To reach out and help one of your blood relatives? *(Beat)* Oh, well I'm *sorry* if you think all I care about is your money, but that is simply not true! I have *never* asked for anything before, never *needed* anything from you before. I've been perfectly self-sufficient, all my life. Now I hit a run of bad luck and I turn to you for help. *(Beat)* What? "*Payback?*" No! Everything I did for you in the past, I did without any strings attached. You knew that. Who came by here to bring you food when you couldn't get out of bed? And who cleaned this filthy, dirty house when you fired all the maids? *(Beat)* No, it was not an "investment" ... how many times do I have to say it? I was doing it because I *cared*! *(Beat)* "For what?" For *you*, you old goat! *(Beat)* How dare you! How dare you call me a liar when I'm only trying to – *(Beat)* Well, maybe you're right. Maybe nobody *could* truly care about you. But if that's the case, then know this, Phinneas: you've brought it all on yourself. If you're so despicable that nobody could ever really "love" you, then *you're* the one who made yourself unlovable ... selfish ... and for what? Really, I'd like to know. What have you gained by being so cruel to those around you? Do you get a thrill from persecuting others, on watching them suffer? Or is it merely some kind of power play, just a game to you? Well, hear this, Phinneas: you won't have to worry about me wanting anything from you, ever again. My "unholy presence" will never again darken your doorway. If *that's* how you want it – fine. Die alone for all I care. Because if I can't be sure of anything else, I can be sure of one thing: you *will* die. Eventually, you too will cease to exist. And from the way you've treated everybody ... I am certain that you will die *alone*.

EMOTIONAL QUICKSAND

HE. *What*?! You're crying *again*?! *(Heavy sigh.)* I *swear* ... sometimes talking to you is like wading into emotional quicksand! One wrong step and – *gulp*! The quicksand swallows up anybody who's around you! *(Beat)* Look, Clarice. I have *tried* to be patient. Patient and understanding. Actually, I can't imagine *anybody* being more patient and understanding than *I* have been for the past six years. I was patient and understanding after I popped the question to you in front of a full dining room at Tavern on the Green ... sitting there and watching, numbly, as you proceeded to sob for two and a half hours. Two and a half *hours*, Clarice! And not only did you use the tablecloth for a hankie, but we never even *ordered* anything to eat! *(Composes himself, then:)* And once again, I was patient and understanding on our wedding day, when you were crying so violently that we had to delay the service ... not once, but thirty-seven *times* ...frankly, I don't know of any wedding ceremony in the history of the world that was delayed so many times it ran into the next day! *(Beat. Calms himself.)* But I put up with all that. All of it, I put up with it and smiled and kept on going ... because I loved you. *(Correction:)* I still *do* love you, Clarice, but I *swear* you have pushed me too far this time! Are you listening to me? Listen, and now hear this: I am *thrilled* to know that we're pregnant – *you're* pregnant! But you have *got* to stop crying! It's been a full week since that test came back positive and your tear fountain hasn't stopped flowing since! How on earth are you going to have this baby, much less nurse it, take care of it, raise it and watch it graduate college?! Well, I'll tell you: you *can't*! It won't work! If you don't come out of that emotional quicksand you're in, this will never work! Now, I don't know if there's such a thing as "Criers Anonymous," but we've got to come up with *something* ... and soon, too -- before you drown this whole household in a torrent of tears!

EMOTIONAL PERSON

SHE. *(Fighting back tears:)* It's not *my* fault I cry a lot! I'm just an *emotional person.* Always have been. My mom says, when I was a baby, I *never* stopped crying. They thought I had the colic at first, but I just turned out to be a crying baby. Then, in school, I got the nickname "crybaby" right away, I think it was the first day of Kindergarten. That name stuck to me immediately and it's followed me around ever since – all the way through my high school graduation ... and into college ... oh, kids are *so* mean. *(Blows her nose, continues:)* My mom says I should've bought stock in Kleenex, she says I've used so many of 'em over the years. My husband thinks I could've gotten in the *Guinness Book of World Records* for the thousands of hours I've cried ... but I can't *help* it! I don't know if I'm just sensitive or what ... things just *affect* me. Like this morning: I went to the donut shop and asked for a dozen assorted. And they said, "we'll give you a – " *(Fights back tears.)* "— baker's dozen!" *(Bursts into tears.)* That was so sweet of them. *(Blows nose, composes herself.)* I know I drive Wally up a wall. *(Laughs in spite of her emotion.)* Wall ... Wally ... hah. That's funny ... *(Trails off and then starts to cry again:)* I've been such a horrible wife ... crying at the drop of a hat ... crying when we got engaged ... crying when we got married ... crying when I found out I was pregnant ... I even cried when I saw our initials together, "W & S Strong," in the phone book! *(Pulls herself together again.)* Like I said, it's not *my* fault, really. I'm just emotional by nature. *(To the point:)* The thing is ... if I take this medication ... I mean, I'm sure you're right, I'm sure it'll stifle my emotions – which means I won't cry as much, I guess – but does that mean I won't *feel*? See, as crazy as this sounds, I'd rather cry all the time than not feel *anything* ... crying makes me know I'm *alive* inside ... if I thought I couldn't *cry* anymore ... *(Beginning to crumble again:)* Gosh, I dunno ... I think that would really make me ... *cry*! *(Collapses into tears.)*

WARNING LABELS

SHE. I wish that life came with "warning labels" ... you know, so that you knew right off the bat all of the bad things that were going to happen to you in the years ahead. As it is now, you just sort of get sideswiped day in and day out with all kinds of wild unimaginables that threaten to rock your world and turn everything upside down! Wouldn't it be great if you graduated from high school with not only your diploma, but also a full disclaimer of all that life had in store for you – all the huge events – so that you could be *prepared* for them? I mean, if somebody had told *me* that I'd be married at 20, pregnant at 21 and divorced at 22 ... well, I'd sure have done some things differently! *(Beat, then backpedaling:)* *Some* things, Rachel ... not *everything*. *(Beat)* Look, I'll admit, your father was a bit of a bum ... well, he was a complete and *total* bum, you know that now. You've seen for yourself that he's ... well, let's just say "unreliable." *(Beat)* And, being his wife, I knew this ... so I tried to tell you up front, because I wanted you to have the warning labels I never had. But I guess having warning labels doesn't mean we'll actually *read* them. Or, if we *do* read them, it doesn't guarantee we'll take them in. Or maybe my whole philosophy is flawed and you have to just experience things as they come. Look, I know I'm rambling here, but what I'm trying to say ... I wanted so badly to spare you any pain. I mean, honey, you are my *daughter* ... and, as far as I'm concerned, you are, like, the best thing that's ever happened to me. Out of all the bad things ... you're the lighthouse that shines over all of everything. I just don't want to see your light dimmed. Not by anybody... or anything.

REVISIONIST LIFE

SHE. I know you're trying to help ... but what you're doing is *not* helping ... it's suffocating! *(Beat)* There's a difference, you know – in trying to guide me along, and live my life *for* me. And that's what it feels like you're trying to do sometimes – change all the mistakes *you* made by living your life over again through me! It's like you're living this revisionist life with *me* as the lead character, it's really irritating. *(Beat)* Mom, I'm not coming down on you ... All I wanted was to see dad. Is that a crime? I know he was a jerk to you, I know he lied to you and treated you horribly – and I fully realize that you and he were like oil and water. But he and I may *not* be oil and water. We may be ... Tang and water. Or not. I don't know yet, but that's the whole point -- I don't *want* to know up front. I want to give it a try, to find out for myself who are my friends ... and who are my enemies. And if he turns out to be an enemy ... fine. I'll deal with it. But I want to be the one to deal with it, not you. *(Beat)* I'm a grown-up now, Mom, in case you haven't noticed ... I'm ready to make my own decisions, take my own chances ... and heal my own wounds. You're right. My heart may get broken. But I think I'm strong enough now to put the pieces back together. At least ... I'd like to be allowed to try. You'll always be my "Mom" ... and who knows? I may come running back for a hug and your wonderful words of comfort ... but let's not decide up front what's going to happen. Okay?

DOMINO EFFECT

HE. No, I'm *sure* you weren't thinking. That's the whole point, Mark: you *never* think! You make all these big decisions without ever once considering how they're going to impact other people ... and what happens? *This. This* is what happens! You re-direct a shipment to Oakland without asking anybody else ... and hundreds of people get screwed – including *me*. *(Beat)* No, no, this is different. Because, when *I* make a decision, I take other factors into consideration. I ask the controllers if it seems like a sound plan. But you ... you just make these sweeping judgments and assume everything'll just work itself out. Well, it *didn't* work out, Mark. You cost us money and you cost us manpower ... and I'm afraid you cost yourself a job. *(Beat)* No, I'm dead serious. You've got five minutes to clean out your desk. *(Beat)* Mark – Mark, no. Don't even start. Appealing to me won't work because I wasn't the one who made this decision. It came from the top. *(Beat)* What? *I'm* a traitor? Ah, I don't think so, Mark. Just because I got promoted and you didn't ... I mean, c'mon! How many times have I covered for you in the past? Huh? Ask yourself that. I've covered for you and made excuses for you and tried like crazy to protect you. Four years now, I've done somersaults trying to keep you safe. But not anymore. You've got to realize, Mark ... every action you take impacts other people. It's the domino effect. And you just toppled all of the dominos in one fell swoop. *(Beat)* C'mon, pack up your things. The clock is ticking. And the appeals are exhausted. You just made your last mistake, Mark. At least, the last one *here*.

LOYALTY

HE. So that's *it*? After all these years? After all the hard work ... all the loyalty? Because I *have* been loyal, Fred. Whatever else you may think about me, I have *always* been loyal to you. *(For example:)* When they came to us in that staff meeting last spring and asked for suggestions for cutbacks, did I offer you up? No, I defended you *and* your team, tooth and nail, do you remember that? Steve and Eddie kept saying we could live without "post sales initiatives," but I fought for you – fought for you like I was one of your own. *(Beat)* Y'know, ever since I took this job, people have slapped my hand. Any decision I've made – *(Slaps his hand.)* – it's always been the "wrong" one. I haven't been able to go to the bathroom without somebody telling me I've peed improperly. Part of me thought, maybe I'd been set up to fail from the very beginning ... and then the other part of me thought that *you* would never let that happen. But maybe the cynical part of me was right all along. Maybe you *were* watching from up on the fourteenth floor, just waiting for me to stumble. Waiting for me to fall, so that you could step forward and announce my defeat. Well, maybe I've lost the battle, Fred ... but I'm not ready to concede the war. You don't like the call I made last week? You could've said something. I would've had time to fix things, to make it work ... but you didn't do that, did you? You let me make the decision and then you waited for it to fail. Like you've done time and time again. *(Beat)* What did you get out of this, Fred? Another promotion? Well, enjoy your life in corporate politics. I ain't playing that game, Fred. 'Cause when you play that game, your friends are always the pawns ... and I won't put *my* friends in that position.

STEEL TRAP

HE. No, you *didn't* buy that when we were in the Bahamas. I'm quite positive. You didn't buy *any* outfits in the Bahamas. You bought a red one that was *similar* to it when we went to Catalina Island. It was a Sunday afternoon and you paid cash for it in that shop that overlooked the water. I think it was around $145. *(Beat)* Well, I remember it because I remember *everything*. I remember all of the things we've ever done ... the places we've gone ... I remember every endearment you've ever whispered to me and all the gifts you've given me ... I even remember all the nasty comments you've hissed at me when you thought I wasn't listening. *(Beat)* And I remember, crystal clear, the day we met. Actually, it's better than a photographic memory, it's more of a *digital* memory. My teachers used to call my brain a "steel trap" because they could write complex equations across the blackboard and I'd instantly absorb every notation. Snap – like a snapshot, committed to memory forever. *(Beat)* So you can imagine, when I saw you outside Leon's yesterday, well ... how *surprised* I was. Because, you were with some guy ... some guy who looked vaguely familiar. And, seeing how I have this digital memory, his face was immediately screened through my data bank ... and there was a match. *(Beat)* No, I *know* you don't want to hear this, but I'm going to say it anyway ... Robby Phelps. You dated him back in college, right? You never did get over Rob, did you? I mean, I only met him once, when we ran into him back in that pub in Hanover. But I remember how you *looked* at him ... I watched you both gaze in each others' eyes and – *snap* – my mental camera filed the image away. And then I saw how you were looking at him *yesterday* – and, *snap* again! And, lo and behold, the two images matched. You and him together. Eyes locked ...smiling ... *(Beat)* So ... what were you doing with him yesterday? And I'd consider my answer carefully if I were you ... because, you see, I have *photographic evidence* to support my claims.

JEALOUS STREAK

SHE. Rick believes that he has this amazing "photographic memory." He thinks he can remember *everything* that I ever did, said or even thought. *(Beat)* Only problem is, he remembers everything *one* way, and I remember it another ... and *I'm* the one who's usually right. *(Beat)* The crux of the problem is, he uses this "photographic memory" of his as if it's some kind of, I dunno, *evidence*. Like, he'll swear I said or did something that I *know* I would never say or do ... and the only way he can prove it is to say, "well, I know that's what happened, because I have this *photographic memory*." He'll say, "you bought those lavender underpants at the Victoria's Secret in Boston, I remember, I was *with* you." But in reality, the real truth is I got them from the K-Mart just down the street before I even *met* him. *(Beat)* Lately he's really started to exhibit a jealous streak. He's, like, "who was that guy you were talking to in the Togo's sandwich line?" And I'm, like, "I dunno, it was just some guy." And he comes back with, "I distinctly saw him sitting on the back row of the Chapel when we got married!" Yeah, right. That was Uncle Albert in the Chapel, who is bald, toothless and decidedly *dead* now. *(Sighs)* At any rate, he thinks I'm fooling around because he saw me talking to *you* yesterday. Yes. Outside Leon's. *(Beat)* I know, I know ... the whole *staff* went there for lunch, but he's got it in his head that we were there *alone*. *(Beat)* Well, I've cooked up this little *scheme*, see how you think this sounds ... I told him that you're my estranged half-brother. My mother's passed on, so she can't refute the story. *(Beat)* I can't tell him we work together, God knows what things he'll start "imagining" about us in the workplace ... what I need you to do is, I need you to show up at the house tonight and ask for me. Let me just warn you: he has a pretty major jealous streak, so if he tries to kill you or anything like that, I want you to have this forged birth certificate on you, to prove that you really are my half-brother. *(Beat)* Oh, no, don't be silly, I'm sure he wouldn't *really* try to kill you ... *(Then:)* But just to be safe, do you happen to have a bullet-proof vest?

SMEAR CAMPAIGN

SHE. *(Angry and mortified:)* You'd really go through with this, wouldn't you? You'd actually *print* this, this *batch of lies* about me ... and for what? *Money?* You went through all this just so that you could sell some damn story and make money off me? *(Hurt:)* Is that all I am to you ... a *story*? After all we've been through? Has this whole relationship been a sham from the very beginning? You know what I mean. You wormed your way into my life so that you could, I dunno, "get something" on me? *(Beat)* No, no you are wrong. You presented yourself as a *friend*. You presented yourself as a confidante. You never *once* hinted at your true motives, and *that's* what makes this so sinful in my eyes. You see, I didn't pour my heart out to a reporter, Simon, I poured it out to a *friend*! *(Beat)* Oh, you really *are* despicable. Fran warned me about you, y'know. She said you were not one to be trusted ... but did I listen to her? No, I listened to my instincts instead. Well, that shows just how dull my instincts have become. I actually *believed* in you, Simon. I actually thought that you were someone I could confide in, someone that I could talk to ... and I certainly did talk, didn't I? Maybe it serves me right for isolating myself like I have ... but I still blame you. You knew I was vulnerable and you took advantage of me! *(Beat)* Well, if that's the way you want it – fire away! Two can play at this game. As you see it, this whole sham is built on the premise that I'll just cave. Well I *won't* cave, Simon. You run this story and I'll swear it's all lies. You're the only one who knows most of these things anyway. You print them and I'll sue you *and* your disgusting tabloid. No matter what you publish and no matter how tall the typeface, I will still hold my head high. So go ahead. Hit me with your best smear campaign, Simon. But I assure you, the mud won't stick to me. Because when all of this is said and done ... the dirt is coming right back on you – where it belongs!

SURRENDER

HE. *(Yawns:)* You know, Julia ... sometimes you are so *naive*. *(Beat)* Yes, I know ... I know that you like to think of yourself as worldly and unreadable ... but you're basically just innocent and simple. *(Beat)* Why? Because. I worked my way into your life with barely any effort and pried your deepest secrets out of you. And here you rant and rave about how you feel "betrayed" ... and I understand that, at least on some level. But you shouldn't feel betrayed ... because only a *friend* could betray you. I was never your friend at all, Julia, that's where you're mistaken. I was only ever here to get something from you. And get it I did. You see, that's what I specialize in, Julia. Getting things. Getting information. Getting dirt on people. You had dirt and I got it. It's as simple as that. I'm not boasting, mind you ... I'm just warning you, don't make it personal. Now, you can threaten me all you want, but your threats don't scare me. I've been threatened by some of the biggest celebrities in Hollywood ... political players ... heads of state ... *they* didn't frighten me. Why should you? You are a big fish in a small bathtub and the plug has just been pulled. The water is going down the drain and you are powerless to stop it. I happen to be the one who pulled the plug and you can either deal with that or you can sit here and complain. Personally, I'd just deal, if I were you. In the end, it's so much more seemly if the fish isn't flopping around in the empty tub, flapping its gills. Don't flap your gills, Julia. It's not attractive. Just surrender. Eventually, this storm will pass and your pathetic little life will return to "normal" – whatever that is. You see, once you look at yourself as a cog in the machine – rather than the machine itself – everything is so much easier. Now ... do we have an understanding?

NEW KID ON THE BLOCK

HE. One of the reasons I've stayed in this job so long is I simply can't stand the idea of being "the new kid on the block" somewhere else. *(Beat)* I know that must sound a bit short-sighted to you, but you have to understand, we moved around a lot when I was a child – I mean a *lot* – and I grew to despise being the "new kid" every place we went. No matter where we moved, I was promptly plopped into a new classroom – ranging from an affluent New York boarding school to a dirt-poor Alabama trailer. Yet, no matter where I wound up ... I was always picked on. *(For example:)* In Seattle, they snuck into the locker room and put Nair in my shampoo – and, after a week of Gym class and showers, I earned the name, "Baldo." In Phoenix, they switched my number 40 sunscreen with cooking oil so that I was quickly broiled to a crisp, giving me the ever-lovely moniker, "lobster boy." In the Delta, they told me there was a hundred dollar bill in a pool of quicksand. *(Beat)* Of course, I didn't know it was quicksand, how the heck would I know what quicksand was? They called me "Sandy" from then on ... not a horrible name, but it tagged me as being naïve and gullible. *(Beat)* Anyway, you can see why I have a bit of an aversion to new places and new people. Here, I finally feel like I've found *my* place ... a place where I'm truly one of the team, where I finally fit in. Honestly, I cannot even begin to articulate how traumatic the thought of your moving away is ... the whole idea of possibly losing you is really quite torturous. But if you only knew the depth of my phobia about this whole "new places" thing ... I can't explain it. Suffice it to say, I can't go with you, Olivia. Not now. I would give anything if you would somehow reconsider and stay here ... but, then again, I'll also understand if you don't want to. All I'm asking is, just try to meet me halfway. I'm a guy who has some problems, sure. But I'm also a guy who loves you. Isn't that worth maybe *not* taking this job in Des Moines? *(Winces.)* Des Moines ... now I remember ...when I was twelve, that's where they nicknamed me "Squirty." *(Beat)* Don't ask.

TEST FLIGHT

SHE. Morton, you can't stay in this rut all your life. You've got to start taking chances. The way it is now, you cling to these limitations that other people have attached to you and those very same limitations become jail bars all around you, like a cell, closing in on you. Imprisoning you. *(Beat)* I'm offering you the chance to get *out* of prison ... hey, think of me as your very own "get out of jail free" card. *(Beat)* Okay, so a buncha kids called you "Squirty" back when you were twelve. Big deal! You're not "Squirty" now, are you? No, I'm not making light of your childhood, I understand perfectly well that you had a rotten childhood ... but that was *then*, Morton. This is now. And your present – your future, too – is whatever you decide to make it. Now, you can stand here and be limited by things other people said about you years ago ... or you can brush all that off and start over. *(Beat)* I'm offering you an opportunity to begin again, Morton. You and me, together. You won't be alone this time, being called "Baldo" or "Farty" or whatever it was. If something horrible happens, I'll be right there. Helping to hold you up ... and needing you to hold *me* up, too. Because, believe it or not, I have horrible days too. There are times when people don't think highly of me, either. But I've learned, I have to push through all that and keep moving. It's the only way, Morton. The only way to survive it is to push through it. *(Beat)* You remember my grandfather, he was a test pilot, years ago. He said that the planes met the most resistance when they were just about to punch through the sound barrier and fly smooth and free. You're feeling all this resistance now, too – but it's time to punch through it all and fly smooth and free. You can do it, Morton. And I'll be here to catch you if you fall. *(Beat)* So, what do you say? Ready to take your new life on a test flight?

DEAD SERIOUS

HE. No! Do *not* touch those chicken bones. *(Beat)* Because! I want to see how long he'll leave them there. *(Beat)* Oh, I'm dead serious. You wanna know something else? I *became* dead serious late last night, when this, this otherworldly insect crawled out of the sink and stared at me. *(Beat)* All right, so maybe it was only a cockroach, but it was a king-sized cockroach and it scared the heck out of me. I nicknamed him "The Hulk," he was so huge. But, you see, he represents a bigger issue than just you and me and the dirty dishes. Because this is about you and me doing all the work around here and Roscoe getting a free ride. Yes, this is about Roscoe! *(Beat)* You know, I wouldn't even mind having him as a roommate if he'd just clean up behind himself once in awhile. But if we fail to step in, it's unbearable ... unflushed toilets, piles of dirty dishes, scummy brown rings in the bathtub – yuck! It's horrific! And the worst part is, we've *spoiled* him by doing all of his housework *for* him. Like some little bratty child, we've spoiled Roscoe rotten because he never has to lift a finger! We lift our fingers *for* him! And now look at the result – Hulking cockroaches and chicken bones all over the counter. Have you ever *seen* so many chicken bones in your life?! That was some monster chicken! *(Beat)* Well, we're going to have to confront him. *You're* going to have to go up there and tell him he's a filthy pig and he's got to change his ways or we're moving out. *(Beat)* No, you *have* to. I know you don't like confrontations, Ned, but he likes you more than me, he'll listen to you. *(Beat)* Don't be afraid of him, what's he going to do, hurl chicken bones at you? *(Suddenly alert, listening to something.)* Shhh. He's awake! I hear him moving around up there. Now. Go. Tell him he's got to start doing his share around this place. *(Beat)* If he refuses to cooperate? Well, then, you tell him he'll be sleeping with The Hulk tonight!

BREAKING POINT

HE. *(Nervous:)* Excuse me. Roscoe? It's, ah … it's Ned. Could I talk to you for a minute, please? I'm … well, I'm not usually very good at these sorts of things, but Earl asked me to come up here and – *(Beat)* What? No, I can't tell which pair of your underwear is clean. They both look pretty gray to me. *(Winces.)* Okay, I'll just look *this* way while you get dressed … *(Turns away, avoids looking at "Roscoe" and continues:)* Anyway, Earl and I were talking about the chicken bones and – *(Beat)* What? Oh, the ones you left in the kitchen. *(Beat)* Well, *I* didn't do it. And Earl didn't do it … so it must've been you! *(Beat)* "Saving" them? For *what*? A voodoo ritual? *(To himself, trying to calm himself:)* Breathe, Ned. Remember to breathe … *(Breathes)* Look, I didn't want to get all worked-up over this, I just wanted to tell you – *Earl* and I wanted to tell you – that – *(Grimaces at something ROSCOE has said and recoils:)* No! I'm not going to sniff the armpit of your shirt! Gross! *You* sniff. *(Shudders:)* Yeah, well, it looks pretty "pitted out" to me. Why don't you just *wash* it? Well, that *is* the whole point, Roscoe, that's the whole reason I came up here in the first place! You've got to start cleaning up behind yourself. *(Beat)* Why?! Because you *smell*, for one thing! Plus, you've left so much garbage in the foyer that it's like crawling through a corn maze for us to get to our rooms! It's not safe, it's not smart and it's not fun! There! I've said it! Wow… I've never asserted myself over anything, my whole life, but you totally gross me out to such an extent, Roscoe, I'm at the breaking point! You have pushed me to the breaking point! No, *I'm* the one doing the talking now! You get down there in your pitted shirt and your grayed-out underwear and you clean that kitchen … *(Turns menacing:)* … or you'll be sleeping with The Hulk tonight! *(Beat)* The Hulk? Oh, wait 'til you see him … he's the biggest cockroach in the Western Hemisphere!

THE LAST LAUGH

HE. *(Whispered:)* They're trying to get *rid* of me – to drive me out of here. It started weeks ago ... each day, they gave me less and less to do in hopes that I'd up and quit. But I refused! I've worked here for seven years now, the only way they're going to drive *me* out of here is in the back of a hearse! *(Beat)* You think I'm just being obstinate, don't you? Of course, you probably can't imagine being demoted from account manager to custodian. That was their latest devious move. For months, they were taking away account after account ... I guess they were hoping I'd be humiliated and quit on my own. But they never realized the depth of my stubbornness! The McMasters account? Buh-bye. The Bolton account? Buh-bye. Yet, even without a premium account, there I sat, like a hibernating bear in my little den, waiting ... waiting for the harsh winter to pass. And then, all of a sudden, lo and behold, the winter got even worse! "Here, here's a mop and a bucket, the men's rest room has pee all over the floor!" *(Looks at his own clothes:)* This janitor's uniform doesn't even fit right. I used to wear $1,200 tailored suits, now I'm stuffed into a $16 pair of coveralls. But I don't care. I'm going to have the last laugh. Did you see how clean I got that floor? Those tiles practically sparkle! You see, it's all a matter of perspective and persistence. First of all, they want to make me miserable ... but I love cleaning. It's my secret fetish. What's more, they think they're going to break me ... but I'm not giving up so easily. The way the executive world works, there's a shakeout every six months or so ... all I have to do is wait it out. It's only a matter of time before all the bastards are gone ... and I'll still be here. Sure, I'll be cleaning these toilets ... but they'll be at home, cleaning their own. The wheels of corporate justice may be slow, Springer ... but they do turn. And one of these days, I'll be back on top again...where I belong!

CHECKMATE

SHE. I don't understand it. We've done *everything* we can possibly think of to make him miserable! You said so yourself, if he got miserable enough, he'd quit! Well, he's not quitting! You tagged him as a quitter – and he's not a quitter! I should fire *you* for mis-labeling him ... but don't worry, I won't. You have far too much dirt on me. *(Sighs)* Honestly, what has this world come to? When you can't force an employee to resign on his own? In the good old days, you could harass, harangue and intimidate people you didn't like into quitting ... but now, thanks to all these new labor laws ... here we are, locked in another hopeless situation! *(Beat)* I think he fancies this a gargantuan game of chess. He believes that he has *me* in checkmate. But he doesn't realize that the *queen (Indicating self.)* is about to make her move. A move that will end the game once and for all. *(Hatching a scheme:)* Here's the plan ... you are to pour a small amount of *oil* in his mop bucket and have Erasmus order him to mop this hallway. The hallway will dry, but the oil will create a slick surface. I will leave my office, execute a spectacular pratfall and cry out in a shrill voice that I've been injured. The water will be tested and it will be revealed that he purposely painted my floor with oil in order to orchestrate my fall in retaliation for his demotion! *(Playing innocent:)* "I didn't *want* to fire him ... the only way to keep him on the payroll was to offer him a different job. I had no idea he was so upset until he carried out this nefarious plot to harm me!" *(Laughs)* Yes! I've still got it! And I'm going to use it to break this little bugger. Break him and get him out of my hair once and for all! Get to work, Morris ... you know what to do, and I expect you to do it!

KARMA BOOMERANG

SHE. I can't *believe* this! I went out on a limb for you, Irving! *(Beat)* Yes, I know. I *know* you have a great resume ... but you did *not* walk in here and land that job on your own – *I* helped you get it! I talked you up to all of the Marketing people, I -- *(Beat)* How *dare* you! Where do you get off, acting like I had nothing to do with it? No, you listen to me – I put my reputation on the line for you. I went in there and swore up and down on your behalf so that you could get a break! And *this* is how you repay me? I can't believe it! Your first official act as VP of Sales is to fire me? *(Sinking into a chair.)* My head is absolutely reeling. I ... I don't know what to say ... I just had no idea that you were capable of such, such coldness ... *(Taken aback:)* You're kidding! Five minutes? Let me get this straight: I've worked here faithfully for three years and you're giving me five minutes to pack up and leave? Well, thanks a lot, Irving. *(Rising with anger:)* I'll tell you what – I will be packed and ready to leave. But you listen to me, and you listen good: trust is a two-way street. I trusted you and you broke that trust. *(Beat)* No, I am not spouting clichés, thank you very much. I am telling you – you throw a boomerang, it comes back at you. You've just thrown a hard one ... and one day, it's going to come back and nail you, right between the eyes. *(Beat)* No, it's not a threat! It's Karma. You screwed me and one day, I promise you, you are gonna get screwed. I may not be around to see it, but I swear, it will happen. *(Beat)* Yes, I'm fully aware that I just lost one of my five minutes. But I lost a lot more than that, Irving. I lost my faith in you. And nothing you ever say or do can replace that. Now, get out of my way. I've got a desk to pack up.

HATCHET MAN

HE. Sylvia, this isn't easy for me ... I hope you know that ... especially since you were the one who helped me out during my "hour of need," as they say. *(Beat)* But ... I'm afraid we're going to have to let you go. *(Beat)* No, I'm very serious. *(Beat)* Please, don't over-react ... I know this must come as a shock to you ... but you mustn't make the mistake of putting too much weight on our relationship. Forgive me for saying so, but I think you're being a bit naïve if you believed that your helping me get this job would protect you in some cosmic way. I'm your boss now – *was* your boss, until a moment ago – and it's my responsibility to assess this team ... to ferret out its strengths and weaknesses ... and to shape it. To prune it. To trim off any extra fat ... any excess baggage ... and you, I'm afraid, are ... well ... excess baggage at this moment. *(Beat)* I'm not trying to provoke you, I'm just saying – *(Beat)* Well, Sylvia, I'm sure there's no need for name-calling. I could've sent a secretary to tell you this, but I did come on my own. I thought I owed you at least that. I don't like being the Hatchet Man, but that's my role at the moment. *(Beat)* Sylvia, it's not some kind of cosmic Karma at work here, it's business. I got a job, you lost a job. I'm not happy about it, I'm not gloating, I'm just telling you ... you've been let go. *(Beat)* You're correct. It was my decision. But that's what leaders do, Sylvia. They make decisions. Even difficult ones. *(Beat)* I'm afraid you won't be able to do that, Sylvia. You have five minutes to pack up your things and then Security will escort you out. *(Beat)* Please don't make the mistake of painting me to be a villain, Sylvia. I'm just a man with a job to do ... and today, *you* happen to be that job.

MY CASTLE

HE. What do you mean, "where's my feet"? Where they *belong* – right there – on the coffee table! *(Reacts to her crying)* Oh, no...What is *this?* *(Points)* I'm talkin' about the tears! Every time I speak my mind, the friggin' waterworks start pourin'outta your eyes like a gushin' geyser! I dunno what's gotten into you, Myra. Lately it's all manners and etiquette with you and I'm just supposed to staple my feet down to some little throw rug and be happy about it? Like the other day. You brought me my can of Vienna Sausages and I popped the top and you grunted and said, "how gross." *(Beat)* Oh, excuse me. "Gauche." Like, what the hell is that, anyway? Italian? *(Shakes his head in disgust.)* "Gauche." *(Beat)* Yeah, well, I don't *care* what it means! This is my castle, Myra! A man's home – listen – a man's home is his castle! Didn't they teach you nothin' in that Catholic school? Maybe some o' them third-world country people's got it right, that the woman is meant to serve the man! D'ja ever think about that? You should be bringin' me my Vienna Sausages with nothin' on but shoes and a smile! *(Beat)* I am not creepin'! I'm just tellin' ya – *(Beat)* What? I'm a *what?* "Cretin"? What the hell is *that* supposed to mean? Look, I don't wanna go around and around with this ... I have spoken, all right? This is my castle ... and I am the king!

FOR BETTER OR WORSE

SHE. You're the *what?* The king? My God, do you hear yourself talk? It's like, the stupidest babble I've ever heard! It's like you're handin' down edicts from your castle turret or something. I can't stand it anymore! What am I to you, some kinda *indentured servant?* When I stood at that altar and said, "for better or worse," I never had any idea how much "worse" it was gonna get! You walk around here like some friggin' patriarch and expect me to wait on you, hand and foot. Well, I got news for you, Roger: this foot is through waitin' on you. It's *your* turn to do somethin' around here. Like cleaning or fixing a meal or taking me out to dinner! When was the last time you even asked me to go out to dinner? And it's not like you even had to *take* me – just to ask if I wanted to go! You wanna know? Two years ago. That's right. Well, then *be* surprised, but that's how long ago it was, I wrote it on the calendar. *(Beat)* What?! Go get the calendar for you? What, am I a dog? Do I play "fetch?" Well, maybe that was the old me, but not anymore. The new me is not a waitress, nurse or babysitter. From now on, you can vacuum your own den and get your own Vienna Sausages. And, yes. I stand by what I said. Vienna Sausages are the ultimate in *Gauche!*

PASSING THE BUCK

HE. I started making excuses very early in life. As a child, I think I pioneered the whole "dog ate my homework" routine. And I didn't even have a dog! I just shredded the blank pages with my teeth and brought in the ripped and tattered corners as evidence. *(Beat)* Ever since then, my skill in avoiding culpability has only increased. *(For example:)* When I set off an M-80 in one of the toilets on graduation day and was caught red-handed in the boys' bathroom, I simply said that Fatty McGee had slipped the M-80 in my Sloppy Joe earlier that day. I'd merely ingested it, I told them, and it came out when I went to the bathroom – I was just as surprised as *anybody* when it went off! And the result? Fatty McGee got expelled moments before he received his diploma ... and I walked away, Magna Cum Laude. *(Beat)* The point is, *anybody* will believe what you're telling them as long as *you* believe it yourself. Now, naturally, it's not easy to convince yourself that an M-80 passed through your bowels and ignited in the toilet bowl. So the easiest way to master this technique is to convince yourself that the other person is *wrong*. No matter what they say – they're absolutely wrong! *(For example:)* "You were late to work today." Wrong. I was not late, I was early. The *clock* was wrong. *(Another example:)* "You took $20 out of petty cash!" Wrong. How do I know that *you* didn't take it? See? It's all about empowerment. Empowering yourself to blame others. My fiancée calls it "passing the buck," but of course she's – "wrong." It's merely defending my own right to not follow through. It's a basic instinct. And I have it down to a science. Now ... are you ready to face your boss? Then let's go. And remember, no matter what he says, he's – *wrong. (Smiles)* Right.

COMPANY MAN

HE. Something's up with Ferguson. *(Beat)* Ferguson, the guy who makes excuses all the time. *(Beat)* He's slipping. Used to be, his lies were completely unbelievable. Now, they're getting more and more remarkably... *pedestrian. (Sighs)* I fear that this is just another sign of the times. That things are becoming more and more mundane around the workplace. And Ferguson is just another example of this, this ... downward spiral. He's a microcosm of the whole company – the whole *world*! This is the question that I put before you today, gentlemen: why aren't we inspiring Jim Ferguson? Hmm? As a company, why aren't we challenging him to lie better? To craft more inventive falsehoods? We should be inspiring our workers to lie, cheat and steal on an unprecedented scale! Theft in the workplace should be soaring to unheard-of levels! But what do we have? Huh? Jones? 3% growth? Record-low sick-day call-ins? What is going *on* around here? When I first started out in the mail room of this company, we stole office supplies like they were going out of style ... embezzlement was at an all-time high, fraud at a fever pitch! We've got to get back to those grand old days when being a "company man" *meant* something! And we're going to start right here, with the Executive Board ... *(Points to one "man" in particular".)* Ledworth. You used to get a thrill out of firing people! I want you to go back to your office after this meeting and fire somebody – fire three people – today! *(Points to another:)* Krauss. You used to boast that you could expense $10,000 worth of business meals in a month. Get on it! *(Takes a deep, satisfied breath.)* Now, then ... now that we've re-set the moral compass of the workplace ... what other business is on the agenda for today?

HITTING BELOW THE BELT

HE. What do you mean, "offensive?" What on *earth* have I done today that could possibly be deemed offensive? *(Beat)* Okay. All right. You got me on that one. I did. I did pick my nose. But hey, big deal. I mean, *everybody* picks their nose, right? Oh, except you. Uh-huh. Well, next time you stop at a red light, look over to either side and I guarantee you, at least *one* of the people next to you will be picking their nose. *(Beat)* So ... what else? What else is it about me that you simply can't bear to be around anymore? *(Beat)* Okay. I do. I do bite my toenails. What's the crime in that? A lot of people bite their nails. *Finger*nails, I know, but toenails are the same thing, they're just on your...toes. *(Offended:)* Now, hold it right there... now you're striking a low blow. You're really hitting below the belt this time. I can't help my dandruff, all right? I have tried Tegrin, Head & Shoulders, everything, *none* of those products work. So what if I have to scrape my scalp once a day ... what is it to you? I don't do it around *you*! I'm sorry if the flakes end up on your clothes, but it's nothing a good quality lint brush won't cure. Honestly. You act as if I'm some sort of disgusting creature that crawled out of a swamp and spewed some vile liquid all over you. *(Taken aback.)* Now, I resent that! I only barfed on you *once*, and that was four years ago! Four years ago and you *still* throw that in my face! Juanita, what is going on here? You used to be charmed by my eccentricities – and that's what they are, eccentricities ... but now you seem put off by me ... irritated by me ... disgusted by me. *(Beat. He saddens.)* Tell you what: I'll stop scratching and picking if it will make you change how you feel about me. I promise. Or, or I'll do it in private. But I swear, you're the most important thing in the world to me. Far more important than getting a good booger. *(Reacts:)* What? What did I *say*? Why are you offended all of a sudden?!

TRADE SECRETS

SHE. My fiancée is the sweetest man in the world ... but he has quite a few ... well, *bad habits*. *(Beat)* Like picking his nose ... chewing on his nails – *toenails*, that is ... and scratching at his dandruff-y scalp all the time! *(Shudders)* I know. It is kind of gross. But underneath all the flaking and crusting and loose skin and ear wax, there really is a great guy. But *getting* to the great guy underneath it all has become more and more ... well, icky. *(Beat)* I didn't notice all these things at first – or maybe they just weren't so bad at first. I mean, he *did* barf on me during our first date, but that was because we'd gone on a roller coaster – and I never remember chronic dandruff being a problem ever during our courtship. I'm talking dandruff the size of Frosted Flakes! *(Shudders in disgust, then:)* At any rate, I just gave him an ultimatum: clean up your act ... or clean out the closet. That's it. I mean it. He's got to get all these fluids and discharges under control – or I'm not walking down that aisle with him! You just get to a point in your life where you don't think nose picking in public is all that charming anymore. That's why I wanted to talk to you, Quincy. You used to be such a disgusting man, but from what I can see, you've really cleaned up your act. I mean, you went from threadbare jeans to tailored suits ... from greasy hair to a crisply-cropped cut. Are there any *trade secrets* you can share with me? Secrets that I might pass on to Tony? I know it's probably none of my business, but anything that you're willing to share – anything – will help. Who knows? Your grooming secrets might even save this marriage!

OLD FART

HE. I remember thinking that my parents were a couple of square old kooks. That they were never "in touch" with what was going on in the *real* world. They consistently scorned anything "new and trendy." They were always aghast at the latest hairstyles, ignored home decorating trends altogether, and firmly believed that polyester bellbottoms would *surely* come back in style one day. I used to cringe in shame when they denounced whatever songs were in the Top 40 and refused to let me play them on my record player. I swore, once I grew up and was a parent myself, that I would *never* be like them. And then ... very suddenly and without warning ... I woke up one day to realize that I've become and Old Fart... and I'm not even *old*! *(Beat)* It all crept up on me, very gradually. One minute, I was hip, hot and happening, partying my brains out at a radical college ... and now I'm buttoned-down, uptight and downright *conservative*! Maybe it was having the kid? I dunno ... but now I see things through my parents' eyes! Isn't that awful? Me, who was the most carefree guy around, now I stay awake nights worrying about the breakdown of the family and the erosion of popular culture. I flinch whenever I see pierced lips ... I groan whenever I glimpse tattooed flesh. I'm my own father, reincarnated! Someone I swore I'd never be like! How does this happen? Was I programmed to turn into him the minute I turned 30? *(The point:)* Mort, you managed to stay so pure ... so true to yourself ... to be who you are without wavering. You're still the exact same guy I knew back in college. So let me ask you ... is there some way to find myself again? Or am I just lost? A prisoner of my own heredity?

YOUNG FART

SHE. Darrel used to be so *fun*. Now he's an old fart. Except he's not even *old*. He's more of a *young* fart. A hunky young guy who doesn't know how to have a good time anymore. *(Beat)* Maybe it was us getting married ... or maybe it was having kids. Me having a baby, I mean, that pushed him into old fartdom. Up until then, he was always ready to party, to have a great time ... now he just mopes. Yeah, he mopes around the house all the time, *worrying* about the future, *worrying* about what might happen, *worrying* about "what kind of world our child will grow up in." You know, the kind of stuff our parents used to say. *(Realizes:)* Unless ... now that we're parents, we just automatically turn *into* worriers. Like, we're genetically programmed, the moment we have kids, to manufacture milk, start worrying and switch into an old fart mentality. *(Beat)* I've tried everything I can think of to shake him out of it. I've taken Noah over to my mother's house for the night and greeted Darrel naked at the door when he came home from work. He spent the whole night *worrying* that it might be too cold over at his mom's. Then, another time, I dug out our old home videos, you know, to remind him of those great trips we took? He just kept going on and on about how unsafe it'd be to take Noah to Europe "in this day and age." Gosh, I thought only our parents said things like, "in this day and age." But Darrel's walking around saying it now ... and, once or twice, I've even caught *myself* saying it. Could this mean ... could it possibly mean ... that we're *both* becoming young farts? I see it in Darrel, but I can't see it in myself yet. Unless I've completely turned into an old fart and I don't even know! Have I? Jenny, have I turned into an old fart? Please. Be honest with me. I'd rather you be candid and me have my feelings hurt ... than to go on being a "young old fart."

TEARS FOR FEARS

SHE. What does it take to make you cry? I've never actually seen you shed a tear, the whole time I've known you. And that *bothers* me. It bothers me a lot. *(Beat)* You see, I *like* to cry. I like to cry a *lot*. *(Laughs:)* I guess that's why you always keep so many Kleenex around, huh? But *you* ... I mean, I *know* you love to laugh ... and I *know* you frequently get angry ... but you never do seem to cry. *(Beat)* Would *pain* make you cry? Like, if I were to stick a needle in your eye right now, would that make you start bawling? Maybe not, huh? Maybe you're the "strong and stoic" type ... Well, perhaps it requires something more personal? Like, if I were to throw your dog in front of a charging freight train, would *that* make you collapse into sobs? I'm just curious. Not that I would actually *do* any of those things, you know ... *(Nervous laugh.)*... I just *think* about them. *(Beat)* Oh, you poor dear. Don't struggle, honey. Those knots are tied very tight, they're only going to burn your wrists if you struggle ...*(Brightens:)* But maybe *that* might make you cry! Rope burns! *(Reacts to something "he" says:)* Oh, you probably think I'm some kind of nut, but I'm really not. My first husband – oh, I never mentioned him? *He* thought I was perfectly insane. But I'm not insane. I just like to cry. That's all. So ... what does it take to make *you* cry, Hector? I mean, I'd love to untie you ... I'd love to set you free ... but I just can't. Not until I see tears rolling down your cheeks. Because then – and only then – will I know that you're the one for me. You see, I *think* you're the one for me. You're funny, you're handsome, you're charming ... but until I know that you can cry ... I can't commit to you. So ... it's up to you, darling. Do you want to tell me? Or do I have to get out the vice grips? It's up to you.

FREAK OF NATURE

HE. I got this ... *problem* with women. *(Beat)* See, every time I start to fall for one, she turns out to be a total freak of nature. *(For example:)* Last year, I dated this one, Natasha. One day, for no reason, she shaves her head. I said, what is that? You look like an egg, but she just laughed and kept talking about Sinead O'Connor or something. Then she started shaving everything in arm's reach: the front yard, the dog, my shag carpet ... it was all really weird. Needless to say, I disarmed her of her shaver and sent her packing. *(Beat)* But the last girl I dated was the most emotional basket case of all. All she did was *cry* all the time. She went on and on, nagging at me all about how she wanted to see *me* cry. Yeah, right. Like I'm the type to break down and sob in front of a date. Anyway, we went out for awhile, coupla months, maybe. She started to get all clingy, you know ... asking me, "will you cry for me?" – stuff like that. I said, I don't cry, baby. I was honest. But eventually, her rubber band snaps. She goes totally wacko. *(To illustrate:)* I wake up one morning, she's broken into my house and tied me to the bed. She's standing over me with a roll of duct tape. "Would you cry if I put this on your hairy chest and ripped it off? Would *that* make you cry?" And I'm like, what the hell is going on? Then she breaks out a pair of vice grips and says she's gonna – well, never mind what she says. *(Beat)* Well, I thought I was screwed, because I hadn't cried since I was, like, seven or something. But I cried *that* day. Thank God, 'cause she turned me loose when the tears started flowing. I bounced her outta there so fast it'd make your head spin. Changed the locks that same night. *(Beat)* What I'm trying to say is ... I like you, Jenny. But you gotta tell me right now if you're a whack-job. 'Cause I don't wanna find out six months down the line that you're insane. You get what I'm sayin'? I don't want there bein' any secrets between us. So if you're a freak of nature ... now's the time to tell me.

WAR OF WORDS

SHE. Ugh! Sometimes you are *so dim*, Thomas! *(Beat)* Because! When I asked you how I looked in my new sweater, you were supposed to say something ... *nice*! *(Beat)* No, no, you *didn't* say something nice, you said I looked "fine." "Fine" is not nice, Thomas, it's what's known as a "passive insult." *(Beat)* "Passive insult." It means you weren't aggressive enough to offer me a *real* insult, so you just cloaked your content in the form of a sub-compliment. *(Sighs, becoming exasperated:)* "Sub-compliment," don't you know *anything*? It means one step below an insult! Honestly, Thomas ... this is very frustrating for me. It's like you and I have entirely different vocabularies! And maybe we do ... maybe men and women just communicate on different levels. I mean, you seem to communicate with burps and farts, while I communicate with a wide-ranging palette of linguistic nuances. But if we're going to have a happy marriage, then you have got to learn to communicate with me! I mean, you're not actually expecting me to sink to *your* level, are you? Because! Burping and farting are *not* communicating. On the other hand, conversing with a veritable universe of words, like I do ... well, that's what I call communicating. See, I can raise you up to my level, but I could never go down to yours. It would be too denigrating. *(Sighs, exasperated:)* "Denigrating!" It means – *(Sighs)* Oh, honestly, Thomas. I don't know what to do with you. Just give me a big belch and I'll know everything's all right. *(Sighs)* It's a good thing I love you ... which means I'd rather hear your belches than not hear your voice at all. Come on. Give me a big fart and let me know everything's okay ... *(Smiles)* There. That's more like it.

COMMON LANGUAGE

HE. Communication. *(Beat)* That's the key to a good relationship. And ... that's what our whole problem is. See, she says I don't know how to communicate with her. She complains all the time that communicating with burps and farts isn't really communicating at all. But I guess it all depends on how you do it. I mean: *(Lets out a big, long belch.)* That says a lot, doesn't it? Yeah! I mean, hey ... a guy can really get his meaning across if he uses his gas in just the right way. But she doesn't see it like that at all! So I've been trying to use words more, you know. Talk to her on her level, with less gas and more talk. But that doesn't work all that well, either. 'Cause she came in here one day last week with what looked like a dead cat wrapped around her, I mean it was the ugliest friggin' sweater I've ever seen ... and she said, how's it look? I guess a good long fart would've done the trick, but I was trying to communicate, see? Now, I didn't want to lie...but on the other hand, I didn't want to tell her it looked like a dead cat either, so I said, "it's fine." Well, you'd've thought I said I hated her guts the way she laid into me. She gave me this whole lecture about how "fine" is not an appropriate compliment to pay a woman, blah, blah, blah. *(Beat)* So that's why I came to see you, Enrico. I'm thinking, maybe we just need a new common language. I mean, if burps and farts aren't working ... and compliments in English don't work either ... well, then maybe if we both learn a new language, that might be the key. Comprende? So ... how much would you charge for three months' worth of Spanish lessons?

LITTLE SPARK OF HOPE

SHE. Poor little Nicholas ... he keeps thinking his mother will come back for him one day. Trouble is, I don't know if that's slightly hopeful or completely heartbreaking. I mean, the jaded part of me just assumes he'll never see her again ... but then there's this little spark of hope somewhere deep inside of me that dreams of them being reunited. *(Beat)* I think about Nicholas and the rest of them, all the time. I lie in bed at night and worry about their problems. *(Bitter laugh:)* You probably just think I need a life, don't you? You always accused me of taking my work home with me ... but that's just who I *am*. I can't simply forget about them and just "assume" it'll all work out okay. Because seven times out of ten, it *doesn't* work out okay. They go home to an abusive father or a negligent mother or a crack house someplace -- and who's there to catch them when they fall? Nobody. I'm the safety net, Alan, I'm the one who's supposed to catch them. If you take me away, they won't have that net anymore, they won't have *anything*! They have so little in this world that they can cling to as it is ... sometimes I worry that I'm their last hope ... their life preserver in a choppy sea. *(Bristles:)* I am *not* over exaggerating my role in their lives! Alan, they need me -- or somebody like me! It doesn't take that much funding to keep this halfway house open -- to make sure there's a place for them! Is that so much to ask for? That there be a place for kids like this? Kids who are not wanted, who are cast aside like old newspapers? They're *people*, Alan. Precious little people who want to grow up and contribute to this world. If you cut back on the program...if you close this place ... that little spark of hope that keeps them going will be extinguished. And if I were you ... I wouldn't want that on my conscience.

COLD, HARD FACTS

HE. You have a very naïve view of the world, Stacey. You think we have bottomless pockets out here in Sponsorland. You think we can just keep doling out money for every imaginable social program on the books. Well, our pockets are not that deep anymore, Stacey. In fact, they've all been emptied. Private donors and local government are not going to pick up the tab for your hobby anymore – *(Beat)* Yes, I do see it as a hobby. I know you think I'm being uncaring and crass and I'm sure this infuriates you, but that's what it is. I'm not saying it's not noble, I mean, after all, you do help several kids each year ... but that's the point: it's only *several*, Stacey. Compared to the tremendous numbers out there that are still suffering, you're only impacting a few. *(Beat)* I know, you're filled with that idealistic mindset, "those precious few could grow up and change the world." *(Beat)* No, I'm not mocking you, but you continually ignore the statistics, Stacey. The cold hard fact is this: yes, you make life better for a handful of poor children. But no ... they don't ever grow up and change the world. None of the kids from this program has ever amounted to anything more than a short-order grill cook. *(Beat)* I know you don't like to see the harsh truth in anything... but it's time you opened your eyes. You're not getting any more funding and the program is not going to be miraculously saved at the last moment. You've got to move on, Stacey. Find another cause. Because this one is dead. And it's time to bury it.

BLIND DATE

SHE. *(Clearly uncomfortable:)* Hi. *(Beat)* My name's Kerri. *(Long, uncomfortable pause.)* Y'know, when I agreed to go on a "blind date," I had no *idea* ... I mean, I didn't *realize* that you would be ... ah ... well ... *(Squirms, trying to be politically correct:)* ... of a "non-seeing-related nature." *(Winces)* Ugh, that sounded pretty clumsy, didn't it? Thank *God* you couldn't see me blush! *(Laughs, then stops herself.)* Ooh, I hope that didn't come out ... well ... *insulting*, it's really not my intent to insult you. I mean, it's not like there's anything *wrong* with being blind, now is there? *(Nervous laugh.)* You probably have other senses that are much more developed than mine, like smell or touch or ... *(Sighs)* Oh, what's the matter with me? Will you *look* at me – *(Winces)* -- ah, I mean, *listen* to me – trying so hard to play the "PC Game!" Why am I so terrified to say it? You're "blind"! All right? *(Holds up 3 fingers:)* How many fingers do I have up? I'll tell you! *Three*! *(Now holds up four:)* How many *now*? *(Then shrinks back:)* Oh ... what is the matter with me? This is all *my* problem, isn't it? I mean, you're obviously very comfortable with your non-sightedness, I'm the one who's stumbling all over myself in the dark here, trying so hard not to offend you and I'm probably being twice as offensive, aren't I? *(Beat, then wounded:)* What? Oh ... well, of course. No, you're right, why bother ordering dinner if it's just going to be a wasted evening? (Hurt at first, then her anger growing again:) I just ... I mean, I never thought I'd be dumped by somebody who couldn't even see what I *looked* like! I'll have you know, I am very attractive, Mister! I have a body that won't stop, and if you choose to dump somebody like me based on something as insignificant as my *behavior*, even before you get to know me, then – *(Apparently, the blind date leaves.)* All right, then. Just don't hit anybody with that cane on the way out! *(Looks around, then:)* Bartender? Another round, please. And this time ... make it a double!

KINDRED SPIRITS

HE. I don't mean to brag, but I've got a sixth sense when it comes to matchmaking. *(Beat)* That sounded pretty cocky, didn't it? What I mean is, and don't take this the wrong way ... I know how to *read* women. Like books. And then it just sort of comes to me who to match them up with. *(Points:)* Take Jeannie, for example. As literature goes, she's pure Tennessee Williams material. Bit of a drama queen ... needs extra attention ... so I pair her up with – *(Points somewhere else:)* Brian. Patient, caring, stable, attentive ... only trouble is, he's blind. But his *qualities* are so right, which makes him the perfect match for Jeannie. I put them together on a blind date, December Fifth. Bingo. They were married, April 3. Let me tell you, he was a hard one to match up, so many women took one look at the cane and sunglasses and freaked. But together? Kindred spirits. *(Looks around the crowd:)* Oh, see Simone over there? Classic Erica Jong. Wants to be the strong one, but secretly wants somebody else to care ... wants to deconstruct all of the men around her, but not be deconstructed herself. I paired her up with Tony. *(Beat)* Nah, he's not here, they broke up last month. Not my fault, by the way. She turned out to be just as I predicted – classic Erica Jong. Unfortunately, *he* was classic Hugh Hefner. Yeah. Go figure. *(Beat)* So ... I'm looking at you, Linda. I'm thinking you're a perfect example of Emily Bronte. Strong, romantic, expressive ... which makes you the perfect match for a guy ... well, a guy like *me*. I'm a romantic, too. I like being strong, but I don't mind if you are. And I appreciate your expressiveness. In fact – *(Shocked:)* What? No! This is not some "line," I'm serious! No, Linda, wait -- wait! Listen! This is not easy for me. You see, the only problem with being a matchmaker ... it's always touchy when the time comes to match *yourself*. Just ... give me a chance. Please? That's all I'm asking. I just have this sixth sense ... that deep down, underneath all the b.s. ... we may be kindred spirits...soul mates...what do you say?

DOG BREATH

SHE. I'm sorry, Keith, I really hate that I have to be the one to tell you this, but your breath is *awful* ... If fact, I don't think I'm exaggerating when I say that you have an acute case of – *(Gasps)* – *dog breath!* *(Exhales:)* There ... I've said it! I've been holding that horrible truth in for *weeks* now, turning away from you whenever you talk to me, trying not to inhale when you whisper sweet little romantic nothings up close, in my face ... forcing you to eat any overpowering odor before we kiss ... even *garlic* is better than your putrid dog breath! *(Feels badly:)* Oh, honey, I'm sorry ... I don't mean to hurt your feelings or anything, but it's really, really bad. *Really* bad. I mean, maybe it's not quite as bad as opening up the lid of a rancid septic tank and dunking your head in a sea of rotten fecal matter ... but it's a close second. *(Brightens with hope:)* But aren't you *glad* I'm telling you all this? I mean, if I didn't love you, I wouldn't *tell* you that you had dog breath! I'd let you go around breathing on everybody and alienating all the people who know and love you. But I *am* telling you ... because I care! And because I want to help you solve the problem once and for all. You have so many good attributes ... you're sweet and kind and very neat ... the only thing holding you back from being a perfect guy is ... well, dog breath. *(Here's the plan:)* But there's hope ... you see, my Uncle Roderick used to have this Great Dane named Gracie with the most atrocious breath on the planet. But after he gave her these special grass-flavored dog bones called Chompees, her breath improved like you wouldn't believe! So ... I bought you a little present, sweetheart! Your very own box of Chompees! *(Thrilled with herself:)* So ... what do you think? I can't wait to watch you "chow down!" So ... what are you waiting for? Dig in!!

NOT MY FAULT

HE. Glum? Darn right I'm glum! You'd be glum too if your girlfriend told you what mine did. *(Points to something:)* Is that thing heavy? *(Back to the previous topic:)* What did she say? She said that I'm *perfect*! *(Beat)* Yeah, she said she loves the way I treat her, she loves the way I talk, she loves the way I act ... she loves everything about me – except my breath. *(Cups his hand and breathes, trying to smell it.)* She said that I have dog breath. She said that it's the only offensive thing about me, but that it's so offensive it makes her run into the bathroom and vomit after I kiss her. *(Cups his hand and breathes, trying to smell it again.)* I never even *knew* it before. Which means, if it really is true, then all the girls I dated prior to Bonnie never told me the truth about my dog breath ... *(Follow me here:)* So, if they lied about that, what else did they lie about? Huh? You know, the things people tell you about yourself are the things that shape who you are ... my mother used to say that. So, I need to know what was true and what wasn't. Only, I have no way of knowing, except -- *(Points to something:)* Hey, is that thing heavy? Do all the cables and things retract, or --? *(Back to the topic at hand:)* Anyway, so now I got this complex about all of my old flames ... like, were they all liars? You know what I mean? So I'm wondering, I mean, I know that's like, police property, but can I rent it or something? I want to give a lie detector test to all of my old flames and see who was telling the truth and who wasn't. Because the truth can set you free. And I need freedom in a big way.

ONE-WAY FRIEND

SHE. I thought maybe if we went to dinner before the movie, we could – *(Stops short.)* Oh. Oh, well, sure, we could always go earlier, that's fine. How about 5:00? We could go over to that place on the wharf that – *(Beat)* Oh, well, that's fine, too. Maybe you could come pick *me* up, since I'm right by – *(Beat, growing irritated:)* No, no, of course, I'll come and pick you up. It's out of my *way*, but ... *(Beat)* Attitude? I don't have an attitude! I'm just sick of being taken advantage of. *(Beat)* What do I *mean*? Look, I have tried to be a loyal friend! And you ... well, Sheryl, I'm just going to say it ... you are a *one-way friend*. *(Beat)* You *are*! Everything is always on *your* terms, it's never on *my* terms, and whenever I suggest my terms, they're always *wrong*! *(Beat)* It's true! Like just now, I said, why don't we eat at that place on the wharf? But no, you want to go to Chloe's. Okay, fine, I'm flexible, I say, all right, let's go to Chloe's. But then you want me to drive across town and pick you up and *drive* you there? Excuse me, do I have the words, "use me" stamped on my forehead? I have tried to always be there for you, y'know? I just happen to be one of those givers who give, give, give ... and now I see that you happen to be one of those takers who take, take, take! You're a one-way-friend, Sheryl! That's the long and short of it! And I prefer not to continue this friendship ... unless the traffic starts flowing in both directions. You get my drift?

MERCY LUNCH

SHE. Jenny, I'm going to be as blunt as I possibly can, all right? Because "subtle" obviously doesn't work with you ... I am *not* picking up the dinner tab, okay? In fact, I am not going to dinner with you at all! Why? Because! I am not your friend! *(Beat)* Did you hear that? Let me say it again: *I am not your friend!* I don't know what it *is* with you, I was only trying to be nice to you that day at work because all of my regular friends were out of town and you looked so lonely. You were always sitting over to the side by yourself eating that paper bag lunch and you looked so ... pitiful. It was a Mercy Lunch! You just looked so sad over there by the Eucalyptus tree and I thought, this'll be my good deed of the day. Well, that good deed has turned into a nightmare! From that moment on, you apparently decided that we were best friends ... you attached yourself to me like a third arm ... like a barnacle ... like a *leech*, Jenny, a luncheon leech – you're sucking the blood out of my lunch hour and I have no idea how to get you off! The way you get *real* leeches off is by burning them with lit cigarettes. *(Losing it:)* Do you want me to burn *you* with a lit cigarette Jenny, is that what I'm going to have to do to get rid of you?! *(Composes herself again, then:)* You call me up and say, "what time are we going to dinner?" And I tell you, very clearly, "we're *not*!" But I guess you don't hear me, because then you come back with, "all right, so then I'll pick *you* up." Well, listen good, Jenny, because this is the last time I'm gonna say it: I don't *want* you to pick me up! I don't want to pick *you* up! I don't want to go to dinner with you! All right? In fact, I rue the day I ever shared that friggin' lunch with you! I – what? *(Oh, no.)* No, no, don't cry, Jenny. I ... I didn't mean to make you cry. I ... *(Sighs)* I'm sorry, I ... hate to make you feel *bad*, I just ... *(Feeling guilty but resigned to her fate:)* Okay ... what time should I pick you up?

SPEED OF LIFE

SHE. What *happened*? I honestly don't know where our lives have gone, it's like they've been sucked up into this big black hole, this cosmic Cuisinart that voraciously consumes the minutes and seconds of our lives. It used to be, we had time to sit down and *breathe*, but now ... every moment's just gone before it even gets here, life seems to go by like a whirlwind. *(Beat, then with meaning:)* She's six, Daniel. Our daughter turned six years old, overnight. One minute, she was a baby, and now ... *look* at her. *(Smiles:)* She always looks so much bigger when she's sleeping, I dunno why that is ... *(Then, a painful realization:)* There are so many minutes I haven't spent with her, so many experiences I've missed ... and for what? So we could have three cars and five bedrooms? Okay, fine. By next year, probably, she won't believe in Santa Claus anymore ... and I never even took the time to enjoy that fantasy with her. I've missed that precious experience that I so loved as a child. Missed it completely. Let it go by while I was busy earning money to pay for nannies who could watch my child while I went back out to earn *more* money. Well, that's what it is, Daniel. We've totally surrendered ourselves to being consumers, that's what our main concern seems to be. Great. She has a nice room and a live-in nanny ... but she doesn't have *us*. I know you're going to think I'm crazy ... but I would give all that we have – all of it – I would give it all away in a heartbeat if it meant I could have those first six years back. Do you ever think about that, Daniel? Do you ever think about simplifying our lives? Because the whole notion – of getting back to basics, somehow, getting back in touch with who we are ... it's begun to haunt me ... and I need to know where you stand.

BIRDS OF A FEATHER

HE. Nicole, I know how you feel ... but you've said it yourself, many times before: *we made choices. (Shrugs)* We decided a long time ago who we wanted to be. Remember? We wanted to *achieve* things in life, we wanted a nice home, we wanted a nice life, we – no, I know, I *know* what you're saying. But c'mon ... you don't *really* want to go back to the "simple life," do you? I mean, you would *never* have been happy in a one-bedroom apartment. Trust me, I grew up in a cold-water tenement and it's no fun at all. The finer things in life require some sacrifice, that's all, and we made some sacrifices. *(Beat)* Don't be ridiculous. We have *not* "sacrificed our child," she has been raised by the best we could hire. She has been lovingly cared for and her every need has been met since the moment she was born. She's lacked for nothing. In fact, I'm willing to bet that these nannies have raised her better than *you* could've. *(Reacts)* What do you mean, I'm being *hurtful*? I'm stating a *fact*! You weren't made to be maternal, Nicole. You were made to eat, sleep and breathe the corporate world. That's what you *do*, Nicole, that's what you've always done! Don't think that suddenly you can shift gears and change your moral compass, your inner being – *(Beat)* What? *(Beat)* No. I don't believe that's "who you were" all along. Because if that's true ... then you haven't been totally honest with me. You always said we were two birds of a feather ... so, it's up to you, Nicole. If we really are two birds ... are your flying days over ... or are they just beginning?

OLD TIME'S SAKE

HE. Benjy Bailey *really* bugs me. *(Beat)* Oh, he's this new guy at my office, he's been strutting around and boasting like crazy about this big deal that just went down -- the McMann merger. Yeah, well, you know me ... I hate strutters and I really hate boasters. But most of all, I hate *liars*. See, *I* was the one who actually built that deal, I orchestrated the whole thing from beginning to end! And then Benjy Bailey walks in at the last minute and claims the victory as his own! Now, I'm not one to "tattle," but I went to my boss, Mr. Corcoran, and told him exactly what had happened ... and he was *totally* condescending! He just smiled and said, "well, my boy, it'll all come out in the wash." I didn't know what to say at first ... but then I took his words to heart. *(The point:)* Now, I know you and I haven't always seen eye-to-eye, Richard. I mean, once we moved away from home, I followed in Mom's footsteps – the corporate world – and you followed in Dad's – the whole biochemistry thing. And I know we haven't exactly stayed in touch all these years, but there are many parts of our childhood that I remember fondly ... and one of the best was the time you created that weird detergent with itching powder in it ... and we put Lanny Lamar's clothes through a cycle in our washing machine ... remember? When you and he ran for Student Body President? And in the middle of his campaign speech, he started itching and twitching and scratching like a cat with fleas! *(Laughs)* Yeah, well, I know you've won countless awards for saving the planet or whatever it is you do here in the laboratory ... but I was hoping maybe you could find a few moments to cook up a batch of that fabulous itching powder. See, Benjy Bailey is supposed to make the final presentation tomorrow. But I'm the only other person on the planet who knows the McMann merger, backwards and forwards. Get the picture? If he were suddenly incapacitated with itching ... well, who would step in and save the day? So what do you say? *(Gestures to himself.)* For your older brother? For old time's sake? I mean, hey ... what's the harm in a little skin irritant between siblings?

BOARDROOM BATTLE

HE. *Sabotaged!* I *was!* I was totally sabotaged! *(Beat, then harboring a grudge:)* And I know just who it was, too ... it was that creep Ed Flynn. I dunno how he did it, but he put something in my clothes that made my skin simmer like I was covered with a heat rash! And in the middle of the biggest presentation of my career! It was so weird, I was up there giving the financial report on the McMann merger when all of a sudden – *(Jolts like something just went up his spine.)* – yikes! There's this massive itch going up my spine! So I say, "excuse me," and reach to scratch it, when all of a sudden – *(Jolts again and grabs his crotch.)* – my underwear felt like it was filled with ants – *fire* ants! Now, I don't have to tell you, most of the board members at McMann are women, so I dunno what they're thinking with me clutching my crotch and gyrating like that. But I try to press on ... when suddenly, I'm seized with a massive itch that engulfs my arms, my legs *and* my neck! *(Re-enacts the event, scratching "everything" in a comic frenzy:)* Yeah, well, I wasn't trying to do a bit of physical comedy up there, I was trying to close the deal. But, in an effort to be a bigger man than Ed Flynn, I excused myself. I hurried to the men's room and scratched and itched like a stray cat in a scratching post store! And at that very moment, the president of the board of McMann, Myron Polymar, comes out of the toilet stall and stares at me coldly. I mean, ice-cube-cold. And he says, in that deep Southern drawl of his, "Mr. Bailey, I believe we're going to be working with one of your peers who *doesn't* have a skin condition." And he leaves! And that was that. I finally got back to my desk an hour later to find out that Ed Flynn sealed the deal. So I cancelled all my appointments for the day and came here. *(Beat)* What'm I gonna "do?" I dunno yet, this only happened a few hours ago, but I'll tell you one thing: he may have won the boardroom battle, but not the corporate war! I am going to find a way to get him, no matter how long it takes. I am going to – *(Flinches, starts to itch again.)* – let me just get this itch first, then I'll deal with Ed Flynn!

LOADED SUITCASE

SHE. I wish you'd unpack your suitcase. *(Beat)* I mean, we've been talking about a, you know, a "permanent" relationship here and it's kind of hard to form a permanent relationship when you won't unpack your things. *(Beat)* It's been seven weeks, Tom. You moved in here seven weeks ago and, well ... I would think, after seven weeks, that you'd want to get out your underwear, your socks, your ear plugs! But no ... that suitcase just sits there in the closet, staring at me like a loaded shotgun ... like, when is it gonna go off? Huh? Like, at any moment, you're gonna pick it up and walk out of here! *(Beat)* Well, that's the appearance you create by leaving a loaded suitcase in my closet. It's like a loaded gun. It feels like you've checked into Extended Stay America and don't want any furniture sent up because you don't plan to live there very long. And do you know how that makes me feel? *Transitional*, Jim. I feel like a transitional step for you, like a stepping stone. And of course, a stepping stone implies being *walked* on – are you walking on me? It seems like you are. It feels like you're stepping on me on your way to God knows where ... and are your shoes even *clean*? The bottoms of your shoes? No, I mean *figuratively*, Jim! *(Becoming unglued:)* Figuratively, are your figurative shoes clean or are you tracking dirt through my house and through my life?! Because right now, at this moment, it's like you're stepping on my face with soiled GOLF CLEATS, and – *(Gets hold of herself and pulls herself back together.)* Well ... just tell me what you want to do with the suitcase, Jim. I'd appreciate knowing if and when it's going to be emptied of its contents.

COMPASS

HE. *Now* I know why I left. *(Because ...)* She's too *possessive*. I think maybe that's what I was attracted to in the beginning, her needing me so badly ... but after a few years, she just got too clingy ... and by that I mean, clinging to me like another layer of skin all the time. I just needed some space. So I split. *(Beat)* Not for good. I mean, it didn't last long ... I was missing her after about a day. But I stuck it out for a coupla weeks. You know, just to be sure. *(Beat)* And then the answer came ... I was missing that other layer of skin. So I went back. *(Beat)* Only trouble is, after a few days, that layer of skin is starting to itch, all over again. I haven't even unpacked my suitcase yet! I keep putting that step off. That's how unsure of everything I feel. And it's like, I'm Dr. Jekyll and Mr. Hyde, there's another me inside of me that I don't know who's trying to get out. I mean, what's goin' on with me? I thought I knew who I was. But now, all of a sudden, I don't know whether I'm coming or going ... or where I'm supposed to be ... it's really weird. And I keep wondering, is my behavior with her symptomatic of something of a bigger issue ... or am I just sick of her? I just feel so lost ... *(Beat)* I remember when I was a kid, I had this Boy Scout compass. And of course, it always pointed north. But one day, Billy McReady stomped on it and from then on, the needle wandered all over the place ... it never pointed north again. *(Beat)* That's how I feel, Matt. I feel like somebody – or *something* – has stomped on my inner compass ... and I haven't been able to find my direction, ever since. *(Beat)* She keeps asking me, are you going to stay? Are you going to unpack your suitcase? And I'm sure that I will ... but finding my direction again ... wow, *that's* gonna be the hard part. That's the thing that's definitely gonna take some time.

KING OF ANNOYING

SHE. What is the *matter* with you? *Nobody* wears a pair of socks until they *rot*! Nobody! Not even a homeless person ... I mean, even a homeless person would aspire to attain new socks! But you, Randall ... I don't know what to say ... you just, you've become the King of Annoying! Seriously. And I don't know if you've *always* been this vile or if it's just me finally waking up to your complete annoying-ness ... but all of a sudden, you're just absolutely – *insufferable*! The disgusting things you do ... like the month-old socks that smell like decaying skunks ... or the glass-breaking belches that echo through the house ... or your using the shower as a *toilet* – honestly! That one was the last straw! I mean, what were you *thinking*, Randall? That women like me enjoy disgusting "guy" behavior? That we're attracted to it? No. We're not – at least, I'm not -- and I thought you knew me better that that. I mean, ever since I've met you, you've been a gentleman ... but now ... it's like you've morphed into an inbred hillbilly with an astronomical gas problem! What would it take, Randall? What would it take to get the "old" Randall back? The kind, compassionate and quiet Randall who smells good and keeps his bodily gasses contained within his body? I'm willing to give just about anything to have you back ... the way you were ... or else, I don't know what I'm gonna do. Believe me. I'm not very attractive with a gas mask glued to my face!

CAVE MAN DEFENSE

HE. You want me to give you a little tip, Boyd? Try being *annoying*. *(Beat)* It works. Trust me, I have seen the light and now I can never go back to being just another "nice guy." What does bein' a nice guy get you anyway, huh? Crapped on? I'd rather be annoying. Which brings me to my point. Y'see, by being disgusting, vile and "icky" – I think that was the word she used – you can get the key to the castle! *(Let me explain:)* Things had gotten pretty … how should I put it? … *uneven* … in our household. Somehow, I had lost charge of things and Doris was ruling the roost, telling me what to do and when to do it! It hit me one day, I had lost full and complete control! Me, the barnyard rooster – completely lost my strut n' scratch. I tried arguing with her, but you know how it is, you or me could never win an argument with a dame. Next, I tried bribing her … you know, buyin' her stuff and talkin' sweet … but she saw right through that. So … I just started being gross. Period. I didn't take a bath, I didn't change my socks, I started lettin' burps fly 24-7 *(Lets a burp go.)* … get the picture? One day, I even let her "catch" me peeing in the shower. I became a total cave man. And y'know what? After two weeks of what I like to call the "cave man defense" … she caved! She *begged* me to go back to bein' the "same old Randall" that I used to be! But I wouldn't give in so easy. I wanted to be sure I'd won, see. So I kept right on stinkin' and burpin' and peein' in the shower and pretty soon, she gets down on her knees and *begs* me … she'll do *anything* if I'll just go back to bein' the way I was. I saw my window of opportunity and I seized it. I said, okay, I'll go back … *IF* … *(Beat)* That's why I can go bowling on Monday, go out drinkin' with the boys on Tuesday, hangin' at the club Thursday and go out golfing on Saturday. Those were my terms. See, she'd rather have the "good" me for a few hours a week than the cave man all the time. It's a win-win situation, Boyd. I see what Kelly's doin' to you … and I heartily suggest *you* try the cave man defense … before it's too late!

ONE-DIMENSIONAL PERSON

SHE. *(Staring in shock at her best friend, who looks totally weird all of a sudden:)* Wow. *(Speechless:)* I ... that's all I can say, "wow." (Beat.) I mean, I knew you were going for a "new look," Stacey, but ... well, I mean ... *(Trying to be nice, but:)* I dunno if that's *quite* it. I mean, it's very ... *unique* ... and you certainly do look like a "new person" ... but you kind of look like a new *dead* person or something. I just never thought of you as the "Goth" type. *(Beat)* Oh, that's *not* Goth? What is it supposed to be, then? *(Beat)* "Nouveau Wicken?" Right ... *(Shakes her head, then:)* Listen, I know you're looking around for a "cause" ... something to make your life meaningful ... but this comes across more like a *fad* than a life's purpose. I mean, what is your *heart* telling you to do, Stacey? *(Beat, then rolls her eyes.)* No, it's *not* telling you to "ditch the planet," where did you even get that from, anyway? Stacey, we used to work side-by-side in the soup kitchen, remember? Volunteering on Thanksgiving Day? You had such a sense of *purpose* in your life, such a desire to help other people ... and now ... I dunno, you just seem so ... well, I'm just going to come right out and say it ... *self-involved. (Beat)* Well, I'm sorry, but I'm *supposed* to be your best friend, I'd rather tell you the truth than stand here and b.s. you. You're turning into a one-dimensional person, Stacey! Someone who's a cardboard cutout, who other people make fun of! *(Beat)* Fine. If that's the way you feel about it. But if you wake up one day and look in the mirror ... and decide to wash out the purple rinse and take all those earrings out ... I'll still be here. Because. That's what friends are *really* about.

EMOTIONAL STRAIGHTJACKET

SHE. All my life, I've felt like I've been laced up in this, this ... emotional straightjacket. My mother was always so prim and proper and I was expected to be all prim and proper ... and dainty ... and perfect ... ugh! It was so frustrating! So, okay. I decided to rebel. I dyed my hair. I pierced a few things. Is that a crime? I got tired of the plaid skirts and the pigtails and I wanted to be something different, I wanted to be *someone* new! *(Beat, then reacts:)* Yeah, well, that's what it *feels* like, Ginny. It feels like you're totally coming down on me. I mean, I know this doesn't conform to what you're used to ... but everything in the world doesn't fall into the way you see things. Some things are different, some *people* are different, and that's what I thought friends were all about – I thought you were supposed to *support* me in the choices I made, not *judge* me. *(Beat)* You are! You are totally judging me, I walked in here and right away you started to come down on me – just like my mother! *(Beat, then surprised:)* What? You sound like you're *threatened* by me ... *(A realization:)* You *are*! You are totally threatened by me! You're seeing in me what *you* want to be and you're just not ready to take the leap – you're not ready to break out of that emotional straightjacket and be who *you* are! You're still living this, this "Stepford Wife" existence – and you're not even a *wife*! *(Beat)* Yeah, well, I think *you* have an inner voice, too, Ginny. And I think, if you listen hard enough, you'll hear it talking to you ... *(Beat)* Look, I decided to shake things up a little, change things around in my own life. And y'know what? It feels *good*. I don't want to see you stay in that straightjacket for the rest of your life. I think it's better to listen to your inner voice and follow it ... rather than look back one day in regret and wish that you had.

KNOW-IT-ALL

HE. It's not *my* fault that I know so much. *(Beat)* If you wish to blame someone, blame it on my *parents* – they were the ones who so vigorously pursued a peerless education for me. Besides, what is the crime? I don't go around, *boasting* about the fact that I went from middle school straight into college ... I don't *boast* about the fact that I designed software packages that revolutionized the banking industry ... I don't *boast* about my I.Q. – *(Beat)* What? Well, that's my whole point. For whatever reason, you seem to hold all of this *against* me. *(Beat)* I know that you think, Margaret. I've heard you talking to your friends, "oh, he's such a 'know-it-all.'" All right. Maybe I am! But what's wrong with being married to someone who's a vast knowledge bank? You could ask me a question on any topic – well, except for sports – and I'd be able to tell you names, dates, facts, amounts ... isn't that handy? Isn't it helpful to have me around? You don't have to go online and "Ask Jeeves," you can ask *me*! *(Laughs, then his face falls.)* Well, then, I don't know what to say, Margaret. You've somehow decided that you're going to be miserable with me. That unless I have a stroke and stop thinking and talking, you're going to feel like you're living a tableau straight out of Dante's *Inferno*. Hmm? *(Recites from memory:)* Alighieri Dante, Italian poet, born in Florence in 1265 – oh! I'm sorry, it was just reflex! You said, "who" – so I told you! *(Beat)* Honestly, Margaret. You've got to find some way to wrap your head around this ... or it will be the death of us. I can try to meet you halfway – try to stop myself from reciting historical references ... but you have to meet *me* halfway, too ... and stop hating my strong points.

PRIMARY FOCUS

SHE. He calls it his "strong point," but I call it being a *jerk*. *(Because!)* He's the *consummate* "know-it-all," he can deliver a lecture on virtually *any* topic at the drop of a hat – whether you want one or not – and it's just so *annoying* sometimes. I mean, how would *you* feel if *your* husband knew everything there is to know about ... well, *everything*? *(Beat)* I know, your Bo doesn't know much about *anything*, but still ... he puts *you* first. I envy that, Connie. See, sometimes I think Gilbert puts his *brain* first and *me* last. *(Beat)* I used to think I was a smart person, Connie. But when somebody mentions Argentina, I'm, like, "what country is that in, again?" – and before I can even dredge it up out of my failing memory, he's already barfing up a detailed report on Argentina's gross national product, it makes me feel like I don't know *anything*! *(Rolls her eyes:)* I know, I know. He said the same thing, he's "handy" to have around ...but time after time, day after day, getting shown up on every topic is really quite wearisome. *(Beat)* When we first met, he was so smitten with me that *I* became his primary focus. But as time went on and he got used to me ... well, then his "old self" began to shine through again. And nowadays we seem to be mired in "old-self-dom" around our house ... and I dunno how to get the "smitten" version of him back. *(Beat)* Provocative underwear? Yup, I've tried that. *(Beat)* Reading the encyclopedia? I've tried that, too. Problem with that one is, I can't *memorize* details fast enough. I mean, I *never* thought I'd say this, but sometimes I wish I were married to a dumb guy. A guy who ... *(Suddenly looks alert.)* What a minute! What you just said! *(Quotes her friend:)* "If he really knows everything, then he knows how to fix this problem." You're right, Connie! If he really and truly *is* an authority on everything ... then he'll have an insight on what we should do! Connie, you're a genius – and, trust me, that's a huge compliment, coming from someone who lives with one!

AFTERTHOUGHT

HE. I never knew I could love someone so much. This beautiful little being, this pure little child ... it was always such a cliché to hear somebody say, "I'd give my life for her." But I know what that means now. The power behind those words. To truly be willing to put yourself in harm's way for another person – and, as long as it protected her, you don't care what happens to you. *(Beat)* I know you can't understand this kind of devotion, Beth. Maybe you don't want to. But you've got to understand, if we decide to move forward ... to become more involved ... to eventually link our lives together ... she will *always* come first. I'm not saying you'll take a back seat or anything like that, but she has to be the first priority. *(Beat)* In my household, I grew up being the last priority. My parents had jobs, social commitments, friends ... and I was always the last entry on a very full dance card. I was an afterthought. Oh, I was remembered on my birthday with a lavish spread of gifts ... and of course, Christmas Day pretended to be "for me"... but I knew that these were merely "obligations." My folks had to make a show of caring for their child on two days of the year. *(Beat)* Maybe that's why I'm so determined to be different. So ... we can continue to see each other ... and who knows where it will lead, I really do want to find out. But not at the expense of my daughter. She comes first ... and will always come first. She will never be an afterthought in my life.

EMOTIONAL SHIELD

SHE. I don't know what to say. *(Beat)* I'm a bit shocked, Damon. After the way things have been going ... they've been going very well, haven't they? At least, I *thought* they were going very well. We were really getting along and you were the one who first mentioned marriage ... and now you're telling me that if we move forward as a couple, I'm officially branded as a second-class citizen. *(Beat)* Well, that's what it *sounds* like. Your child is more important than me ... that's what you said. No matter what happens between us, she will always come first? I know I sound like a shrew, but I'm not trying to be insensitive. You care about your daughter. Of course you do, who wouldn't, it's only natural to love your own child. But I thought we meant something to each other, the way you talked – *(Beat)* No, I am not trying to put words in your mouth, but I am deathly afraid that you're trying to use that six-year-old as an excuse to pull away from me. You are! You are hiding behind her, like an emotional shield! Suddenly we're starting to get close and you get scared and, "well, my daughter comes first," that's just a passive-aggressive way for you to pull away without actively pulling away! *(Beat)* Well, say what you want ... and believe what you want. But I refuse to be a second-class citizen in anybody's life. Even yours. So decide now. Is there room for me in your life – and your heart – or should I walk away now?

MY PEACE

SHE. I can't stand it anymore! Every word he says is like ... fingernails across a chalkboard! All he has to do is say, "good morning," and it's like – *(Imitates the screeching sound of fingernails across a chalk board.)* It's *horrible*! I mean, I know I'm not a perfect picture of patience ... but all he's got to do is *look* at me and I'm mad as hell, all over again! *(Takes a breath, calms.)* I'm sorry, I didn't mean to explode, it's just that this house is so small and with him lying in there on the sofa bed, I feel trapped sometimes ... I keep thinking that somehow, this'll get easier ... but it just gets worse and worse. And y'know, I blame myself in some weird way. Can you believe it? *He* was the abuser all those years ago, and I blame myself for hating him. *(Beat)* This is hard, Don. You know how hard this is for me ... how I've struggled with this ... Sometimes, I just wish he had suffered like I did, in some way, *any* way ... that he somehow knew my pain because he'd experienced it himself. But all that he's done is prosper! In every aspect of his life, he's excelled, while I've struggled for everything I've achieved. He's never even really offered me a helping hand – my own father! *(Softening:)* You're the only good thing that's ever come into my life, Don. Sometimes I wonder how I found you and why I even deserve you ... but then I realize that he's the villain here, not me. I should be entitled to goodness, shouldn't I? I mean, me of all people, why should my life be bereft of goodness? I've got to find a way to get out from under his spell. And I think maybe the only way to get there ... is to forgive him. To finally and fully forgive him, once and for all. Then – and only then – will I find my peace.

BROKEN

HE. George, can I talk to you for a second? It's about Lana. *(Beat)* What? No, no, she doesn't *hate* you, she ... *(Beat)* Okay. All right. Look ... enough games. Maybe she *does* hate you, George. There, I've said it. How does it sound? Is that what you expected me to say? I know it's what you've suspected all along. And it doesn't take a genius to see why. What you put her through as a child? *(Beat)* No, it *is* my business, George, she's my wife now ... and you're my father-in-law, so like it or not, it *is* my business. Especially when you come here and stay under my roof and try to manipulate her. You made her life a living hell all those years ago, and you wonder why she doesn't throw her arms around you now in some big love fest now? *(Here's why:)* She resents you, George. She resents you for what you've done to her and for how you've ignored her all these years and for how you've never taken responsibility for your actions – even now. You've let her bear the brunt of your abuse and the weight you've thrust on her shoulders ... well, it's almost broken her. *Almost. (Beat)* But, you see, George, she's stronger than you ever realized. Because she will *not* be broken. And she will not be bought. You can't just waltz in here with a big smile and an expensive present and think that everything's okay. Because, in doing so, you're treating the symptom. Not the cause. The cause is who you are – and what you did – all those years ago. And until you can face that and come clean ... well, then, of course she's going to hate you. I don't blame her, George. And I swear, if you ever do anything else to hurt her ... you're gonna have to deal with *me*.

PAYBACK

SHE. Marshall, I wish you could get a life. *(Beat)* I really do, I wish you could just walk into the "life" store and buy one off the rack. But, unfortunately, you can't. You have to make a life for yourself ... and that will take some time and some effort. *(Beat)* Hello?! Are you even *listening* to me? Marshall, you have to get up off this sofa sometime ... and get back in the game. I know ... I know she broke your heart, I know it feels like she ripped it out and stomped all over it, but you can't give up. Marshall, don't bury your head in the pillow. Listen to me, I know what I'm talking about ... because! Older sisters just know these things. Besides, what kind of a sister would I be if I didn't tell you the truth, huh? C'mon, Marshall. You've seen me depressed and bottomed-out thousands of times ... I always bounced back. If I can make a comeback, then surely you can, you've *always* been stronger than me! *(Sighs sympathetically:)* I know. I *know* you wanted to marry her ...I know she was "the one." But ... well, obviously she wasn't really. I mean, you caught her red-handed with Larry Swanson. C'mon ... how could it have been "meant to be" if she was telling you she loved you but she secretly had the hots for Larry Swanson? *(Beat)* I am not rubbing it in! I'm trying to make you *laugh*! I'm trying to bring you back from the brink of despair! C'mon, Marshall ... you were always so good at lifting me up when I was down and out ... won't you let me do the same for you? Well, I think it's time for payback ... so I'm not leaving here until you smile. I'm dead serious. If it takes all night ... if it takes a week ... if it takes a whole month ... you're stuck with me until you wake up out of your funk.

FIXING A HOLE

HE. You can delude yourself all you want. The answer is no. *(Beat)* You think you're being a "good sister," but do you know what you're *really* being? A pain in the ass. That's right, Sheryl. You're standing over me, telling me things are going to get better ... well, you're wrong. Because. I *know* they're not going to get better. I just found the only woman that I ever loved in the arms of Larry Swanson ... his toupee tangled up in her engagement ring – which *I* gave her – and she didn't even feel guilty about it! If I hadn't caught her, she would've kept right on seeing him, the only reason it's even an issue is because I caught her! *(Beat)* Man, oh, man ... I didn't even see this train wreck coming. I mean, you think you know a person ... like I knew her ... all she ever expressed for Larry Swanson was contempt. She laughed about his fake hair! *Laughed*! And – what? Just because he has more money than I do ...? Oh, my God. It makes me sick just to think of it! Larry Swanson! LARRY SWANSON! *(Sinks down into a chair, suddenly exhausted.)* Please. *Please* don't think you can cheer me up, Sheryl. I'm beyond being cheer-up-able. I've passed cheer-up-able ... and I'm where I belong right now: in despair. So take your cheery and upbeat attitude elsewhere. You're not going to cheer me up, Sheryl. This I promise you. I just need to feel miserable for awhile, until I don't *feel* miserable anymore. I know you want to help ... but this is one instance where you *can't* help. This is a broken heart, Sheryl ... it's sort of like a cold, it needs to run its course. I know all this, *intellectually* ... but I'm still miserable. So let me just be miserable for awhile, okay? It's not your fault that you can't fix it. It's just that some things ... don't need fixing. Some things eventually fix themselves ... if you just leave 'em alone.

ROCKET SCIENCE

HE. Eddie, I swear! I am trying to teach you somethin' here. But you don't know the first thing about the fine art of horse racing 'cause you don't listen to nobody else! First rule above all else, ya gotta listen! *(Let's go over it again:)* I told you, ten bucks on Two Bits and you put two bucks on Buck Wheat. And *now* what have we got? Nothin'! You lost the last five bucks we had! *(Beat, then brightens on hearing something:)* What? You got money left? How much? Okay ... well, then here's what we'll do ... you go back up to the window and put two bucks on Three Blind Mice to Win and three bucks on Terrible Twos to Place. And then your last dollar on Bottom Dollar, if you want, *or* you could put the last one on Been There, Done That to Show. You got all that? *(Sighs, exasperated.)* Eddie, it's not that complicated. It's like you don't understand a thing I tell you! What am I speakin' here? Egyptian!? *(Looks up:)* Now look! We've missed the second race. Great. We'll have to wait and bet on the next one ... *(Consults a form:)* Okay, here's what we'll do, so listen up and listen good, this is your last chance to get in good with me: go up to the window and put three on Four-on-the-Floor to Show, two on Win, Lose or Draw to Win and ... how much you got left? *(Beat)* What do you mean, you don't know?! This is not rocket science, Eddie! We're bettin' on horses! Any idiot can walk up to the window and place a bet! Okay, okay, fine. I'll do it. Just who are we bettin' on again? *(Beat)* What are you laughin' at? It's all your fault! You've got me all confused now!

TRUST UNCLE LARRY

HE. People in the family are always tellin' me, "trust Uncle Larry," but ever since I started trustin' him, things have gone horribly wrong. *(As if to explain:)* He lost all my money at the track, crashed my car, burned down my apartment, maxed out my credit cards, got me beaten up twice and took my shoes. Do you have any idea how hard it is walkin' home at four in the morning with no shoes on? That's why I gotta sit. I can't stand up 'causa all the glass cuts on the bottoms of my feet. All thanks to Uncle Larry. *(Beat)* Weird thing is, whenever I try to tell anybody about how much trouble Uncle Larry is causin' me, they just laugh and smile and say, "you gotta trust Uncle Larry!" Yeah, well, all that *trust* has made me broke, homeless, carless and now I got my feet cut up. I can't even walk over to work to get my paycheck ... which is my *last* paycheck, by the way, 'cause Uncle Larry got me fired. On account of he came to visit me and threw his lit cigar in the trash. Only he missed the trash and it landed in the secretary's hair. And she's the boss's wife. So you can imagine how happy *he* was to meet Uncle Larry. *(Sighs)* I dunno what I'm gonna do about this Uncle Larry thing. I keep tryin' to be nice, but you see where it's getting' me ... I know trust and family are supposed to be important parts of life, but maybe in this case, I could use a little less trust and a little *less* family. Know what I mean?

YOUR OUT

HE. I always thought that I had a sense of purpose in life. Focus. Vision. Direction. But then I met you and I have to admit ... I'm a *loser*! *(Beat)* I mean, talk about a sense of direction, nothing stops you! You practically walk through brick walls! Here I was, feeling pretty good about my lot in life, but after spending some time with you, I now look at myself like a completely washed-up hack. No, it's not just losing the job, it's everything. What I've accomplished ... what I've done with the time I've had ... I guess you tend to re-think your life when you have lots of time to sit around. *(Beat)* I'm not feeling sorry for myself, I'm just saying ... I wish I'd done some things differently, that's all. Like ... doing something that meant something to the world. I could've found a cure for a rare disease or published medical journals that brought healing information to sick people or been a missionary and changed people's lives for the better. But what did I do? Design the daffodil pattern for disposable paper cups. *(Beat)* It's easy to say, "it's never too late," but I'm too weary to start over, Annie. I know that might sound like a cop-out to you ... and who knows, maybe in time I'll find that inner sense of purpose again. But right now, I need to stew in my own self-loathing. So I think maybe we'd better call it quits. Nobody wants to be around self-loathing. So ... I'm giving you your "out" here and now.

NEVER TOO LATE

SHE. So you lost your job ... big deal! You said you hated that place anyway! Now's the time to rise up and be a phoenix. Isn't that the creature that comes up out of the ashes and gets reborn ... or ... something, I don't really remember my mythology all that well, if that even is mythology. What I'm saying is, it's never too late to reinvent yourself, Richard. It's never to late to give it a shot. I hate to see you close in on yourself, you have such tremendous potential to do great things. I know you feel beat up and tired at the moment ... well, who *wouldn't* after working at a mind-numbing place for years? I think you need some time to rest ... and recuperate ... and then formulate what it is you want to do with the rest of your life. *(Beat)* No, I do not sound like a self-help seminar! Richard, believe it or not, there is a "rest" of your life, Richard. A lot more out there ahead of you, just waiting for you to grab hold and explore. *(Beat)* I'd like to be the one who explores it with you ... however, I'm not going to pressure you, or suffocate you. You just tell me when you're ready to get out the road map of life and start the journey. I'll be here, waiting. Because I think we make one hell of a team ... and we could take one hell of a journey together.

MIRACLE

HE. Some people might write it off as mere coincidence ... but I know that it's much more than that. I knew you were coming to me, before you ever even appeared. *(Beat)* The car rolled over Teresa ... skidded off the highway and landed in a ditch where it was completely buried in snow. With me pinned inside. For two days, I lay trapped in that car, freezing ... and praying. Praying my brains out ... for a miracle. I was half out of my mind with fear and half out of my mind with hope ... but before I lost consciousness, a sense of calm fell over me and I saw a face ... nobody I knew ... the face of a beautiful, beautiful woman. A week later, I came to in a hospital room in North Dakota ... and that very same woman, that beautiful woman I saw in my dream, was standing there, at the foot of my bed. *(Beat)* Of course, we both know now, you had walked into the wrong room. *(Beat)* Or *did* you? Yes, you were looking for your sister's room ... but somehow, in some strange way I can't explain ... you were led to me. (Beat.) I should've died in that car, Teresa. But I didn't. I held on, something *made* me hang on ... and that's because I knew you were coming. *(Beat)* I used to be the kind of guy who relied on cold, hard facts. But something happened that night that pulled me out of the world of facts ... and plunged me in a bright new world of miracles. *You* are my miracle. How else can you explain it?

GRAIN OF SALT

SHE. I don't know what to say. He thinks I'm an answer to his prayers. *(Beat)* No, don't laugh, Debra. He really believes that I was sent to him. Me. Can you believe it? *(Beat)* Well, you can roll your eyes if you want to ... but it's actually very flattering to think that you're an answer to someone's prayers. He thinks he saw me in a *vision* ... and I think ... well, I don't know what I think. *(Beat)* You probably think he's crazy ... or that he's just coming on to me or something ... and there's a part of me, too -- that cynical part – that wonders if he's just some kind of freak. But then there's another part of me that wants to believe him so badly. I mean, c'mon, Debra ... we don't believe in anything. None of us do, we're all so jaded and angry and so ridiculously steeped in attitude ... that's right, consummate "New Yorkers." We scoff at anything joyful that comes our way. I look at myself and I realize, I've turned cold, hard and negative ...I didn't used to be that way. And now, here comes this pure soul, this remarkable man filled with love and hope ... and I want to buy into that. I really do. I want hope in my life again. I know you think that's sappy or silly or selling out or whatever ... but I don't think I care anymore. Used to be, your opinion mattered so much ... but now I've seen a light ... a light in his eyes ... that I want to bask in. Nobody's ever looked at me that way before. And I don't want to lose it. So you can believe what you want and think what you want ... and you can hate him if you want. But I've finally found a source of goodness in my life ... and I'm not letting it go.

SHORT PLAYS FOR EVERY VENUE

JUDGMENT CALL AND OTHER PLAYS
Frederick Stroppel
This collection of darkly comic one-acts by the author of *Single and Proud and Other Plays* includes *Judgment Call, Soulmates, Chain Mail, Perfect Pitch* and *Coelacanth*. (#12658)

ISRAEL HOROVITZ: 5 SHORT PLAYS
Free Gift, Speaking Well of the Dead, Three Weeks After Paradise, Security and *A Mother's Love*, five dramas written in the aftermath of September 11th, are included this collection by the prolific American playwright. (#21973)

OFF-OFF BROADWAY FESTIVAL PLAYS / 27
Born to Be Blue by Mark Bellusci, *The Parrot* by Le Wilhelm, *Flights* by Susan Cameron, *A Doctor's Visit* by Mark Loewenstern, *Three Questions* by Maurice Martin and *The Devil's Parole* by Eric Giancoli were winners in the 27th Annual Short Play Festival. (#17706)

THE KUKKURRIK FABLES
Oscar Mandel
Forty-two playlets for two to ten actors combine wisdom and whimsy for auditions, show fillers or full evenings of Aesop-like tales with a modern twist. (#13060)

SHADOWBOXING
The Shadowbox Cabaret Theatre
Twenty-two outrageous sketches provide an eclectic mix of comic gems, some of the most successful material ever performed at the renowned Columbus cabaret. (#21461)

TEN-MINUTE PLAYS FROM ACTORS THEATRE OF LOUISVILLE /Volume 5
Edited by Michael Bigelow Dixon and Michele Volansky
Foreword by Jon Jory
Twenty-five short plays by some of the most exciting dramatists writing today are included in this volume. The series is popular for classes and showcases. (#22275)

For the broadest selection of short plays in print, see
THE BASIC CATALOGUE OF PLAYS AND MUSICALS
online at www.samuelfrench.com

SHORT PLAYS FOR EVERY VENUE

THE BEQUEST by Dale Wasserman
Eyebrows rise in a small town when a notorious playboy dies leaving a large bequest to the lovely wife of a local reporter. "A polished miniature from a playwright better known for his blockbusters."—*What's On*. 3 m., 3 f.(#4267)

CELEBRATION by Harold Pinter
Diners and the staff at an elegant restaurant treat audiences to some unusually entertaining fare in this London hit by a major voice of the modern theatre. "[An] entire smorgasbord of gorgeous verbal moves."—*New Yorker*. 5 m., 4 f. (#5870)

THE JUICE OF WILD STRAWBERRIES by Jean Lenox Toddie
A woman seeks renewal after loss in this touching play. "This gem celebrates life, love and the wisdom that comes with age."—Mill Mountain Theatre, Roanoke. 1 m., 1 f. (#12659)

MOSQUITO DIRIGIBLE AEROSOL DEODORANT by Conrad E. Davidson
A professor who thinks he is a dirigible undergoes other transformations during therapy, even becoming a mosquito. Unfortunately, the psychiatrist has an obsessive fear ... of mosquitoes. 2 m., 2 f. (#15732)

REFUGEES by Stephanie Satie
The hearts and minds of new immigrants and refugees as they reinvent their lives in American are revealed in five scenes that are set over five weeks in an English as a Second Language class. 1 f. (to play 3 m., 7 f.) (#19773)

SLAVERY by Jonathan Payne
In the 1030's, the Federal Writer's Project interviewed former slaves who were then in their eighties, nineties and older. Here are some of these moving, first-hand narratives. Paired with traditional Negro spirituals, they offer dramatic insights into the human side of slavery. 3 m., 4 f. (#21521)

For the broadest selection of short plays in print, see
THE BASIC CATALOGUE OF PLAYS AND MUSICALS
online at www.samuelfrench.com

Recently Published One-Act Plays

THE AWARD AND OTHER PLAYS
Waren Manzi

One for the Money
Moroccan Travel Guide
The Queen of the Parting Shot
The Audition
The Award

CHERRY SODA WATER
THREE RELATED ONE-ACT PLAYS
Stephen Levi

Cherry and Little Banjo
Red Roses for My Lady
The Gulf of Crimson

CONTACT WITH THE ENEMY and GETTING IN
Frank Gilroy

DECISIONS, DECISIONS
Fred Carmichael

GENDERMAT
Mark Dunn

GUARDING THE BRIDGE
Chuck Gordon

LUNACY: A BATHROOM TRILOGY
Richard Tuttle

The Lunatic from Number Seven
Sing a Pretty Song
Search and Rescue

OFFICE SUITE
Alan Bennett

A Visit from Miss Prothero
Green Forms